MANAGING TO INSPIRE

Bringing Out the Best in Those You
Supervise

Also by Bob Sullo:

Teach Them to Be Happy
The Inspiring Teacher: New Beginnings for the 21st Century
Inspiring Quality in Your School: From Theory to Practice
Activating the Desire to Learn

MANAGING TO INSPIRE

Bringing Out the Best in Those You Supervise

Bob Sullo

iUniverse, Inc.
New York Lincoln Shanghai

Managing to Inspire
Bringing Out the Best in Those You Supervise

iUniverse books may be ordered through booksellers or by contacting:

iUniverse
2021 Pine Lake Road, Suite 100
Lincoln, NE 68512
www.iuniverse.com
1-800-Authors (1-800-288-4677)

The views expressed in this work are solely those of the author and do not necessarily reflect the views of the publisher, and the publisher hereby disclaims any responsibility for them.

ISBN-13: 978-0-595-43171-7 (pbk)
ISBN-13: 978-0-595-87514-6 (ebk)
ISBN-10: 0-595-43171-2 (pbk)
ISBN-10: 0-595-87514-9 (ebk)

Printed in the United States of America

For Frank Ferguson. It took some time, but you finally have the book you envisioned. Thanks for the inspiration!

CONTENTS

▼

Acknowledgments

I am grateful to the hundreds of supervisors who have taken time during workshops to share their frustrations and successes. I have tried to include your collective wisdom and address your concerns on the following pages.

Dr. William Glasser continues to teach me as I help individuals and organizations move towards increased quality.

I am most indebted to Frank Ferguson, President of Curriculum Associates. Without Frank's encouragement, I never would have undertaken this time-consuming but exciting and enriching project. As I worked through draft after draft, there were times I was ready to give up. Frank said, "I think you have a book that can help people develop more successful companies. I want to help you get this book in their hands." I am forever grateful for his unfailing belief in the value of *Managing to Inspire*.

Every author needs another set of eyes and a skilled editor. I am fortunate to work with Ernesto Yermoli, who makes my writing more crisp, concise, and clear without compromising content.

Finally, my wife Laurie gives me the freedom I need when I get "lost" in a project. Her unconditional support is remarkable.

Bob Sullo
Sandwich, Massachusetts
January 2007

Foreword

I have held paying jobs for more than sixty years and have encountered wonderful people who presided over thriving, nurturing organizations. I shall always be grateful to those who helped me and on whose shoulders I stand. It is my hope that you will make your organization one of those caring, nurturing places that enriches the lives of every employee. If that is what you want, *Managing to Inspire* will help.

As a company, your goal may be to provide quality products and services that make life better for those who use them. Companies are largely defined by what they value and how they act—by the way they "walk the talk." *Managing to Inspire* will help you clarify what you value and ensure that you align your action and beliefs.

Although our company has long practiced lead management and collaboration, until now we lacked a written guide to help us on our unending journey to become "super good" lead managers and supervisors. *Managing to Inspire* contains a great deal of helpful advice and guidance for managers and supervisors who want satisfied, self-directed, productive employees.

Managing to Inspire is ready to assist you in becoming "super good ... and getting better!"—as we often say at Curriculum Associates. I trust that you will find Bob Sullo's guiding hand and wisdom as valuable as we have.

Frank Ferguson
President, Curriculum Associates, Inc. 1976–2007
President, BOSE Corporation 1969–1976

Preface

The 1980s rock n' roll hit "Working for the Weekend" captures an unfortunate truth: most employees do not especially enjoy or value their jobs. Their all-too-obvious goal is to do enough to make it to the next weekend, holiday, or vacation. For these employees, quality is not found in the workplace; they believe that work is something to endure, not celebrate.

Do you want your employees to be working for the weekend, or do you want them to love their jobs and help the company thrive? Imagine what it is like to be working a job that is empty at best, day after day, week after week, month after month, year after year. Bringing out the best in others is an essential characteristic of a successful leader. When you inspire your employees, their lives are more meaningful and enjoyable—and your company gains an important competitive advantage.

For over 20 years, I have consulted with employees and managers from around the country. Although some of us work in small companies and some in large, we all want a productive, successful workforce. We can create work environments that are more conducive to quality performance than the ones we have today. The choice is ours.

Managing to Inspire is based upon the principles of internal control psychology and lead management. I wrote this book to help you manage more effectively by bringing out the best in those you supervise. While it is fashionable to talk about "quality" in the workplace, such discussions are frequently superficial. Everyone wants quality. Let's take the discussion beyond that obvious cliché; let's make the concept of quality in the workplace specific enough to apply in our day-to-day interactions with people at work. Let's make it "real" enough that work becomes more satisfying to managers and employees alike.

Much of what you will encounter in this book flies in the face of conventional wisdom. I plan to challenge you and invite you to challenge yourself. Conventional practices will lead to more of the same: too many failing companies, too many frustrated supervisors, and too many employees doing just enough to get by. If you're satisfied with that, this book has nothing to offer. If you're looking to distinguish yourself as an inspirational leader who helps employees find satisfaction in doing high-quality work, read on.

CHAPTER 1

▼

WHOSE LIFE IS IT, ANYWAY?

Do you believe your mood is "created" by what happens to you, or do you believe you are in control?

Personal responsibility is a major component of internal control psychology, which asks people to reflect upon and evaluate their behavior. Those unfamiliar with internal control psychology sometimes worry that it is not compatible with the world of work. "This may be appropriate in some settings," they say, "but I could never use it with my employees. My job is to evaluate their performance. Asking employees to evaluate their own performance is a recipe for disaster." Rest assured, applying the ideas of internal control psychology is not a recipe for disaster. In fact, it gives you, your employees, and your company an opportunity to achieve greater success.

There are a number of variations of internal control psychology. I highlight choice theory, developed by Dr. William Glasser, who has written extensively about the theory and its application in a variety of settings. (For more information, I encourage you to consult the bibliography at the end of this book.) I have applied choice theory in my personal and professional life for over 20 years. Because choice theory is a fully developed theory of human behavior, it explains behavior in every situation, including managing employees and building a successful organization.

Most managers have had some training in psychology. Unfortunately, the majority are only familiar with *external* control psychology. This carrot-and-stick approach may be adequate when the goal is simple compliance, but today's complex world requires employees to engage in high-quality work.

Getting the best from your employees requires a thorough understanding of human behavior. Internal control psychology helps us accept responsibility for our lives. The following two stories illustrate what I mean.

Karen's Story

I have known Karen for decades. She is a competent, dedicated teacher. Laughter, joy, hard work, and academic excellence characterize her classroom. Students leave much more competent than when they enter and they enjoy themselves along the way. This does not mean there are no upsets or difficulties in her class, but Karen views these as opportunities to grow and develop greater competence. When all is said and done, students in Karen's classroom become more responsible, more skilled, and better educated.

Many years ago, I noticed that Karen seemed less energetic and joyful than usual. I asked how things were going and mentioned that she seemed "down." Karen's comments were revealing.

"Once the corridors are filled with kids," she said, "my energy will return. It's magical. I see the kids and I feel much better. It just happens to me and I have no control over it. They make my day!"

I suggested to Karen that the good feelings she experienced when she saw the students didn't "just happen" and weren't "magical," but were the result of choices she made regularly as a dedicated teacher. I wanted Karen to accept responsibility for her success. Even though we had known each other for years, Karen ended our conversation with the comment, "I'd rather see it as just magic."

Melanie's Story

My daughter Melanie was seven years old and in the 2nd grade when she was asked to participate in a group piano lesson. Melanie preferred private lessons; she was not comfortable performing in front of others until she felt competent. Several days before the group lesson, my wife told me that Melanie seemed concerned about the upcoming lesson and asked me if I would speak with her about it.

I began by asking Melanie, "So what's the story with this lesson?"

She looked at me and answered, "There's just something in my head and I'm choosing to be nervous about this."

Choosing to be nervous! Here was a seven-year-old taking full responsibility for her feelings and her life, even something unpleasant. I will forever treasure the memory of my young daughter taking full ownership of her life and her feelings.

Melanie discovered at a very young age that she creates her own life. While that does not mean that things, both good and bad, won't happen *to* her, it does mean that she controls her life much more than most people realize. That knowledge will help her live her life to the fullest.

Conclusion

Whose life is it, anyway? Karen lives as if she is not responsible for her joy. She believes it "just happens to her," that she has "no control over it." She fails to take ownership for her success. Karen sees the world in a way that separates her feelings from her actions. How many employees do you supervise who remind you of Karen, competent and successful, yet living as if life "just happens to them"? Imagine how much more successful they will be when they learn that they are the architects of their personal and professional lives.

Melanie's story is a celebration of life. She accepted responsibility for her uncomfortable feelings. As I continue to learn from her, I watch her take ownership of her many successes as well. She is fully alive and it is a pleasure to be in her presence. I have no doubt that she will be the internally motivated, successful employee all managers dream about.

Looking at the world from the perspective of internal control psychology involves a fundamental shift for many people. It demands that we accept total responsibility and allows us to experience what it means to be fully human. In this spirit, I invite you to read, reflect, and evaluate.

Reflection

As you read this book, you will discover that you "choose" how to feel, even when the feelings are uncomfortable or painful. Thoughts and feelings that are habits seem like they happen *to* us, yet we are always making choices. Do you agree?

Chapter 2

▼

Internal Control Psychology

Would you be a more effective manager if you had a solid understanding of motivation and behavior?

Why Begin with Theory?

Managers are busy, so they like to cut to the chase as quickly as possible. Less patient readers would prefer to jump immediately to a discussion of effective management strategies and skip the theory. Yet practices based on a valid, well-understood theory tend to endure, whereas those without an articulated and internalized theory to support them almost always fail.

A strong foundation provides strength and durability. Just as a house must be supported by a strong foundation if it is to last, if managers hope to succeed they need a strong theoretical foundation: internal control psychology.

Making an Investment

Learning a theory is like any other investment. Consider the investment you made when you became a manger. Some of your colleagues who made different choices enjoyed a short-term advantage. They had time to earn overtime pay while you paid for courses or immersed yourself in job training that gave you the skills you needed to assume a leadership role in your company. Although there are exceptions, statistics suggest that those who invest in education and job training will be financially better off over time.

Learning internal control psychology will take some time. It will take even longer to integrate it into your personal and professional life. Managers who master a few strategies without the support of theory may be better off at first, but creating a quality organization is more like a marathon than a 100-yard dash. The greatest success is reserved for those who invest wisely.

Choice theory explains how and why we behave the way we do. The easiest way to introduce it is by starting with a discussion of external control psychology, with which you are no doubt already familiar.

External Control Psychology

External control psychology is based upon the following two fundamental principles:

1. When you observe a behavior that you wish to *increase* in frequency, reward or reinforce that behavior.

2. When you observe a behavior that you wish to *decrease* in frequency or even eliminate, punish that behavior.

External control practitioners prefer to use positive reinforcement over punishment; indeed, many current practitioners eliminate virtually all mention of punishment. Regardless, their theory is based upon the assumption that people are *externally controlled*. They believe that our behavior is shaped by rewards and punishments. A manager who practices external control will reward or sanction employees, believing that this builds a successful organization.

Choice theory, on the other hand, is based upon the belief that people are *internally* motivated, driven by powerful instructions built into our genetic structure. The outside world, including all rewards and punishments, only provides us with information. It does not control us or make us do anything.

External control psychology and internal control psychology are as far apart as any two theories can be that attempt to explain human motivation. While external control psychology may be effective in getting employees to be compliant, it never inspires the high-quality work that is the hallmark of the most successful companies. Yet because external control psychology permeates our culture, many of us accept it as truth without giving it much thought. If you want to successfully manage your employees, I implore you to think about these issues more seriously than you ever have before.

External control psychology is most strongly linked to B. F. Skinner, who often stated emphatically that freedom is an illusion (Watson, 1930). For those who cherish a democratic society based upon the principle of freedom, Skinner's assertion demands careful scrutiny:

- Do you wish to propagate a theory of human behavior that is contrary to the notion of personal freedom?

- Do you accept a view of humanity that reduces us to reactive creatures, equally capable of being programmed through the systematic administration of rewards and punishment as a computer or robot?

- Do you agree with Skinner that freedom is an illusion? If I have no freedom, is it fair to hold me accountable for my actions?

For too long, these fundamental questions have been brushed aside. External control psychology continues to be taught in universities and has permeated our most basic social structures, including our families and our workplaces. But how can we hold employees responsible for their actions if they are nothing more than reactive creatures, shaped by outside events? I can only be held responsible for my actions if I am free, if my behavior represents a choice. It is a philosophical contradiction of enormous proportions to maintain that freedom is an illusion, but suggest that people are responsible for their behavior. Amazingly, most people in our society continue to champion this contradictory logic!

One of the unintentional but significant byproducts of a belief in external control psychology is an increase in irresponsibility. People working for managers who systematically dispense rewards and punishment see themselves as out of control, believing their success or failure is attributable to people and things outside of themselves. Such an attitude is as pervasive among successful people as among less successful ones. People who are told that their supervisors "make" them perform become adept at excuse-making and externalizing, blaming others for their failures at work and at home.

Our behavior is motivated by universal psychological needs that are internal, not external. With a thorough understanding of choice theory, you will discover that we are free and can reasonably expect people to behave responsibly. The concepts of freedom, responsibility, and accountability provide dignity to us as human beings and exciting possibilities for those who manage others.

Our Basic Needs

We are born with specific physical and psychological needs, and we behave in an attempt to satisfy these needs. In addition to the well-accepted physical needs related to survival (hunger, thirst, warmth, etc.), we have four basic psychological needs that must be satisfied if we are to be emotionally healthy:

1. Belonging or connecting

2. Power or competence

3. Freedom

4. Fun

When people have satisfying, effective behaviors to meet their needs, they typically abandon less responsible, less effective behaviors. Our goal as managers is to help our employees develop appropriate behaviors that contribute to the success of the organization as they continuously strive to meet their basic psychological needs at work.

Let's consider each of the basic psychological needs separately.

Belonging or Connecting

The need to belong or connect is what drives most of us to live in groups. We are social because of our need to belong. Most of us enjoy connecting with others and being part of a larger system. The need to belong is what leads us to join teams, groups, and civic organizations.

Work can be an environment where managers and employees alike follow the drive to connect responsibly in a way that benefits both the individuals and the organization.

Power or Competence

We often think of power as something we have *over* other people. In fact, power involves competence, achievement, and mastery. Our genetic imperative is to achieve, to master new skills, to gain competence, and to be recognized for our accomplishments. The universal human genetic instruction to be competent and to accomplish is especially important for managers.

Managers who believe in external control psychology have trouble believing that humans are genetically instructed to achieve. Consider some of the amazing things humans have created—our telecommunications network and the Internet, for example, or the medical breakthroughs that are announced with numbing regularity. We create because the genetic instruction to expand our capabilities burns in our minds and hearts. When working hard satisfies the need to achieve, employees will work hard.

Skilled managers remember that everyone wants to develop skill and competence. Be sure to nurture that need in your employees. As you help them discover healthy, responsible ways to increase their sense of personal power, they will be less driven to get power "over" others in destructive ways and more likely to become powerful by making valuable contributions to your company.

Developing competence helps us satisfy our inborn need for personal power—something essential to create satisfying, meaningful lives. Being successful at work is one way for people to build a satisfying life.

Freedom

Making decisions and having choices is part of what it is to be human and is one reason why we have been able to evolve, adapt, and thrive. One of our jobs as managers is to help others follow their genetic instruction to be free in a way that is responsible, respectful of others, and supportive of the organization.

When people hear about the need for freedom for the first time, they may become uncomfortable, fearing that freedom implies a laissez-faire attitude. In truth, some rules enrich our lives and structure is helpful to most of us. In most cases, we do not need to provide our employees with more freedom. What is crucial, however, is that those we manage recognize the many freedoms they do have. Employees who perceive themselves as relatively free are not excessively driven to satisfy that need. Those who perceive themselves as having insufficient freedom, on the other hand, behave to get the freedom they believe they lack.

Most managers give their employees ample opportunity to satisfy the genetic instruction to be free, but may not make this sufficiently clear to their employees. While it is essential to establish parameters in the work environment, our employees can meet the need for freedom at work.

Fun

Just as power is best understood in a general way that encompasses more than simply competition, fun involves the wonder, excitement, and joy we experience whenever we learn anything new. The connection between fun and learning is important in workplaces: the most enjoyable work experiences are those that involve the greatest learning and lead to the greatest productivity. Successful managers make work an enjoyable place where employees follow their genetic instruction to be playful, have fun, and make new discoveries that help the organization flourish.

The Quality World

While our genetic instructions are universal, each of us is unique. Our individuality is conceptualized by something choice theory refers to as the "quality world."

We are born with basic needs, but our quality world is empty at birth. Through need-satisfying interaction with others, we gradually construct our unique quality world. Everything that we place in this world relates to one or more of the basic needs. It is precisely because this person, possession, activity, or value is need-satisfying that it becomes part of our quality world. In our quality world we have idealized versions of everything: the perfect partner, the perfect vacation, the perfect meal, the perfect business plan, the perfect work relationship, the perfect job.

Quality World	*Basic Needs*
• People	• Belonging
• Possessions	• Power
• Ideas	• Freedom
• Values	• Fun
• Beliefs	• Survival

We all develop quality world pictures for each of the basic needs. Some pictures relate to multiple needs. With my wife, I am able to easily meet each of my basic needs. She is a person I love and to whom I feel connected. I meet my need for personal power in our relationship, not because I have power "over" her, but because *with her* I can be competent as a husband, parent, and professional. I am freer in my interaction with my wife than anywhere else. I have fun and learn from her regularly. Because we are able to follow our genetic instructions successfully, we have a satisfying marriage.

How does this relate to you as a manager? Your employees bring their basic needs to work with them every day. If they can be connected, competent, free, and have fun while they are at work, they will put working for you and the organization into their quality world. Because work will be need-satisfying, they will exert maximum effort and do high-quality work. Work will become an important part of a meaningful, satisfying life.

We work for those things that we believe enrich our lives. People put enormous energy into volunteer organizations, civic groups, or churches without being paid a cent. Why? Because these activities and what they represent enrich us in ways that money alone could never do. People don't work just for pay—a point that is lost on those who create elaborate incentive programs for high-performing employees.

Think about how you manage. Do you inspire your employees to put working hard into their quality world? Do you threaten with sanctions and entice with incentives? Do you help your employees derive a sense of personal satisfaction from contributing to the organization? How you manage will determine if your employees settle for competence or strive for quality. When you manage so your employees want to work hard and be successful, everybody wins.

We Create Our Reality

What we call "reality" is the world we experience—the *perceived* world. Even though objective reality exists outside of us, we each create our own reality based upon sensory input, current knowledge, and personal values.

Our sensory systems modify and distort information coming from the real world, at least to some degree. Sports officials make calls based upon what they see. Supervisors treat their employees based upon what they see and hear. Our clients have expectations of what we will do based on what *they* see and hear. Regardless of "accuracy," our perceptions are impacted by what our senses inform us to be "true."

Incoming information is screened against our existing knowledge. Sometimes we have sufficient knowledge for input to be accurately perceived. For example, when I am driving my car and I see that the rear lights of the car in front of me are glowing bright red, I know from past experience that the driver has applied the brakes. This knowledge serves me well and I choose to apply my own brakes as a result.

Even when our information is flawed or insufficient, we still create our perception of reality. Imagine that your company needs supplies. You have been asked to research prices and make a purchasing recommendation to your supervisor. You make your recommendation without knowing that one of your company's four regular suppliers routinely grants a 2% discount. Although your recommendation will be based on incomplete information, it will reflect your understanding of what is "true," accurate or not. Effective managers ensure that everyone has easy access to all relevant information so that decisions are based upon accurate perceptions.

Incoming information is also screened against our personal value system. We are constantly bombarded with input, and as far as we can tell, much of it has very little impact upon us. This information is assigned a neutral value with very little or no distortion involved. For example, as I drive to work I am aware of other cars on the road. Almost always, this information is of little consequence and neither pleases nor displeases me. Under these conditions, I assign a neutral value to the information. If, however, I become aware that a car I see is being driven erratically and poses a possible danger, I perceive it quite differently. In other circumstances, a car may be perceived positively. For example, if I were broken down on a sparsely traveled road and in need of assistance, the sight of another car would be valued positively because it would represent a chance to get help in a difficult situation.

The more strongly we value something, either positively or negatively, the more likely we are to perceive it differently from others. Effective managers are aware that their values impact their perceptions. They also appreciate that the values of their employees might lead them to perceive a situation differently even though everyone "heard" the same story and was given the same information.

In summary, we take information in from the real world through our senses, understand it based upon our existing knowledge, and evaluate it based upon our personal values. Whether the reality I construct matches the real world experience or not is largely irrelevant: I will behave based upon the perceptions I construct.

The Comparing Place

Our brain constantly compares the picture of how we *want* things to be at that moment, and our *perception* of what is real at that moment. We automatically assess how closely they match. If they are reasonably similar, we get an internal signal that things are going well, at least for the moment. On the other hand, if the two perceptions are sufficiently different from one another, we get a powerful internal signal telling us something is wrong.

Imagine you are conducting a sales presentation to a group of potential clients. You are keenly aware that if you bring in just a few more clients, your company will be well positioned to become a major force in the industry. During your presentation, you notice your audience nodding in agreement and exchanging looks with each other that suggests they are impressed. They ask the expected challenging questions, but your answers demonstrate that you are competent and the product you are offering provides genuine value.

Your perception of what is happening as you present closely matches your quality-world picture. You get a strong positive signal and you continue to present the material in much the same way, your confidence growing by the minute. If however, your perception of the presentation differed substantially from your quality-world picture, you would get a strong negative signal, and would likely change your approach.

The process of internal self-evaluation helps us decide if what we are doing is effective. Change occurs only when I come to the conclusion that what I *perceive* is so different from what I *want* that it is worth the effort required to behave differently.

To change my behavior, I must either change *my perception*, perhaps because new information has been introduced, or I must change *my quality-world picture* so that what I perceive no longer adequately matches what I want.

The internal signal drives our behavior. If it indicates I am getting what I want, I continue to behave in much the same way. If I am pleased with how my employees are performing, I will continue to manage the same way. If my marriage is going well, I will continue to conduct myself the same way in that relationship. If I drive a golf ball down the middle of the fairway, I will strive to maintain my swing.

I am still driven to behave when the internal signal is negative, but because of the negative feedback I am getting, I behave differently. Generating alternative behaviors is preferable to continuing to act the same way with the same unsatisfying results.

It is helpful to remember that all behavior is purposeful, and that everyone is doing the best they can. Not all behavior is effective or responsible, but *it is always purposeful*. Go back for a moment to the hypothetical sales presentation. Pretend that things were going horribly, that there was a huge discrepancy between what you had hoped for and what was taking place. Regardless of what you choose do when you make the evaluation that the presentation is not going the way you want, your choice is always made with the idea that the new behavior will help. Your effectiveness will be determined by the behaviors you have available to you (everybody is doing the best they can). Throughout our lives, we try to find effective ways to act when there is a discrepancy between what we want and what we perceive.

Total Behavior

All behavior includes the following four components: acting, thinking, feeling, and physiology. When you change any one component, the other components change as well.

Total Behavior

- Acting

- Thinking

- Feeling

- Physiology

To illustrate the concept of total behavior, let's go back to the story of Melanie and her piano lesson in Chapter 1. The evening after we spoke about the piano lesson, I asked Melanie if she was still "choosing to be nervous."

"Oh, no," she said. "That's all over now."

Melanie's comments perfectly illustrate the concept of total behavior. In her own words, she was "choosing to be nervous." Nervousness represents the *feeling* component of her behavior. Although it is difficult to feel better simply because we want to, when we experience an unpleasant emotion we behave to help us feel better. When I asked Melanie how she stopped "choosing to be nervous," she identified the *acting* component of her total behavior: "Well, talking about it last night really helped." She then brought up the *thinking* component of total behavior: "Also, I spent some time thinking about what we said, and when I went to bed I just thought about how I didn't need to be nervous."

Melanie initially referred to the two components of behavior over which we have most direct control: *acting* and *thinking*. She then brought in the *physiological* aspect of total behavior when she said, "And it seemed that after I had a good sleep, I woke up and didn't feel nervous anymore." A refreshing sleep altered Melanie's physiology, impacting the other components of her total behavior.

The purpose of behavior is to help us *feel* better. Paradoxically, we have little direct control of our feelings. It's hard to feel better just because we want to, or to feel more ambitious simply because we want to. However, we have control over our *acting* and *thinking,* two other components of total behavior. When we significantly change our acting or thinking, our feelings and physiology change as well. In Melanie's case, the conversation we had (acting) and the reflection she did (thinking), coupled with a good night's sleep (physiology), ameliorated her nervousness (feelings). It is usually preferable to focus your effort on acting and thinking, because they are the components of behavior that we can consciously change with the greatest ease. Even though it is sometimes difficult to change our acting and thinking, it is almost always easier than trying to change our feelings and physiology directly.

The concept of total behavior is important and powerful. It allows us to take ownership of our lives. Once Melanie realized that "nervousness" was a choice she was nonconsciously making, she was able to make a more satisfying choice. She was no longer a prisoner of her feelings.

Once you understand and internalize the concept of total behavior, you will gain greater control of your life and take responsibility for your actions. A headache will no longer be something you just "get." It is the physiological component of a total behavior that you *can* control, at least to some extent. Customers will no longer "drive you crazy." Employees will no longer "push your buttons." You will discover that even though things happen, you remain in control and choose how to act at each moment. You can always act and think in ways that maximize your success, both personally and professionally.

Conclusion

Behavior is always purposeful. We behave in an attempt to create a match between what we want and what we perceive. The process of acting, perceiving, comparing, and acting is never-ending as we continually strive to connect, to be powerful, to be free, and to have fun.

A solid grasp of internal control psychology in general, and choice theory in particular, is essential because it explains behavior and motivation. It affirms that human beings are active, not reactive. It teaches us that we are internally motivated, not controlled by outside events or stimuli. It refutes the carrot-and-stick model of understanding human behavior (external control theory). With a firm understanding of choice theory, we can build workplaces consistent with the notions of internal motivation and personal responsibility.

Reflection

As a manager, you will be well served by learning and applying internal control psychology. You will understand that you can't *make* your employees do what you want. You can, however, create a work environment that enables your workers to satisfy their needs by doing the kind of work that will make your company more successful. Employees who find work need-satisfying are more productive.

Supervising from an internal control orientation will increase your effectiveness as a manager.

Managing involves interaction. Understanding what motivates your employees will help you do your job better—and to enjoy it more.

CHAPTER 3

▼

LEAD MANAGEMENT

Do you spend too much time telling your employees what to do and how to do it? Do you wish they would assume greater responsibility? Would you like them to be internally motivated at work and take pride in what they do? This chapter will help you develop useful strategies.

Supervisors perform multiple tasks: ensuring that those they supervise work productively to achieve the organization's goals, mentoring new employees, addressing problematic behavior in the workplace. Regardless of the specific "hat" I may be wearing at any given time, I will be a more effective supervisor when I implement management strategies based upon internal control psychology. Because this approach involves leading others (as opposed to bossing them), it is called *lead management.*

As a lead manager, I continually assess whether my actions match my picture of who I want to be as a manager. Every interaction with my employees provides choices. Some situations are best managed by routine supervisory action; others require that I mentor new or struggling employees. Occasionally, I may need to address poor performance or counterproductive behavior. After considering the situation and determining what is appropriate, I choose those behaviors that help me become the manager I want to be.

Lead management is made up of two components: the *relationship* between the manager and the employee, and the *process* used when interacting with others. Let's examine them both in detail.

The Relationship

Successful managers create a positive connection with their employees. Even though they are task-oriented, lead managers appreciate and value the human element and build relationships that demonstrate genuine *caring* for their employees. They communicate to their employees that they are interested in helping them achieve success and the satisfaction that comes with being a competent, productive worker.

Effective lead managers make sure their relationship with employees remains professional and appropriate. The *rules* of a relationship are substantially influenced by the *roles* we have relative to each other. For example, when I accept the role of "consultant," you have certain expectations of me. How we relate to each other during our time together will be determined to a large extent by our respective roles.

Defining a positive relationship is particularly important in the workplace. To effectively manage our employees, we need to build a strong connection with each of them. At the same time, managers must choose behaviors appropriate to and consistent with their role. Having a strong relationship with your employees does not mean you need to become best friends with them; in fact, it is better that supervisors and associates *not* be best friends.

Managers function as supervisors, teachers, and coaches. The relationship between managers and employees is not one of equals. Ideally, the manager and the employees like each other, value each other, and respect each other, but the relationship differs from pure friendship because there is a legitimate power differential between the manager and those being supervised. There is a difference between being friendly and being friends. Lead management suggests that you be friendly with your employees; it does not imply that you be friends with them.

I encourage you to take time to clarify your vision of a successful relationship between a manager and an employee. This is an opportunity for you to develop *your* quality-world picture of an appropriate supervisor-employee relationship. The specifics will vary from manager to manager, because we have different personalities and styles. What is essential is that we each identify our vision of an appropriate work relationship with those we supervise. If you cannot imagine the relationship that leads to the greatest job satisfaction and productivity, you will never be able to create it. You must be able to clearly visualize your goal to choose the behaviors that will take you where you want to go.

Identify a productive work relationship for all your professional connections. Think about an appropriate relationship with your supervisors and with other managers within the company. Create your picture of a relationship with customers, vendors, bankers, shareholders, and other stakeholders in your corporate world. Even though you cannot control how anyone else behaves, this process provides you with a blueprint for how to conduct yourself in every important work relationship—an essential step in taking personal responsibility and being a successful lead manager.

Present-Tense Orientation

Lead managers focus on the present, making sure that "every day is a new day." Our objective is to help employees become more competent and productive, regardless of past success or failure. Of course, being focused on the present does not mean that we ignore the past, which remains important when it actively impacts the present. Imagine, for example, that one of your employees regularly uses sarcasm with others, including clients. Even though this habit began in the past, it continues in the present and is unacceptable at work. An effective lead manager will address this issue.

The past is also worth revisiting when it represents an area where someone has been successful. There is no reason to reinvent the wheel each time a problem is encountered. Let's say you are supervising an employee who is struggling with his job responsibilities. Rather than simply threatening the employee—a typical management strategy based on the carrot-and-stick model—it is helpful to ask, "How did you resolve the problem the last time you encountered something like this?" This question does two things: it identifies the issue as a problem that needs to be addressed, and it suggests that the employee has the resources to overcome it. Even if the *exact* strategy used in the past is not appropriate this time, past successes can be used as building blocks in current situations. A lead manager equips employees with skills to solve their own problems.

Bosses who practice external control routinely remind employees of past failures, convinced that bombarding others with a litany of their shortcomings will make them more productive workers. Lead managers have no interest in berating others, because it only serves to perpetuate failure. This is not the way to bring out the best in your employees.

Think of a time when your past failures were brought to your attention, perhaps with sarcasm, at least with disapproval. You already knew about your shortcomings and learned nothing helpful when reminded of things that you could not go back and remedy. How did you feel at that moment? Did those feelings help you become a better employee?

In most cases, emphasis on past failure is counterproductive. It is more productive to focus on the *present*, helping our employees develop competence *now*. Rather than revisit a past they can't change, effective lead managers stay grounded in the present and help create a better future.

Don't Let Problems Overwhelm You

An unfortunate reality is that some of our employees have personal histories replete with failure. Some have had to deal with an inexplicable death of a family member; some have lived in poverty; others are surrounded by crime, drugs, and other difficulties. Still others were raised in homes where there was little love and affection expressed in a healthy way.

Successful lead managers are not overwhelmed by these unfortunate stories. It's not that we don't care; it's that when we allow ourselves to be overwhelmed, we sacrifice our ability to help people forge a better life. I have heard people say, "It's no wonder she doesn't do her job very well. Look at what she has to endure every day when she goes home! It's amazing she gets to work at all." The problem with comments like this is that they unintentionally perpetuate the cycle of victimization. People need our *strength and help* to make things better. Pity feels good for a brief period, but it will not help anyone escape the victim box. Provide structured support and help your employees experience the success they so desperately need to create a better life for themselves.

Accept No Excuses for Irresponsible Behavior

Lead managers never accept excuses for irresponsible behaviors. This does not mean you refuse to listen to a reasonable explanation—there are times when all of us have legitimate reasons why we cannot do what we expected to do. People *do* get sick. Cars *do* break down. Unforeseen circumstances occasionally arise and the practitioner of lead management accepts these inconveniences.

An excuse is when someone creates a rationale designed to abdicate responsibility. Remember: lead managers help employees develop responsible behaviors. When we accept excuses for irresponsible behavior, we perpetuate irresponsibility and may even communicate that we never really expected our employees to act responsibly. In an effort to be nice, we exacerbate the problem.

Avoid Criticism

Even though lead managers do not accept excuses, they avoid criticizing employees. Criticism is an especially damaging behavior, though one used routinely. Unfortunately, there is such faith in the value of criticism that we sanitize it by calling it "constructive criticism." Criticism is one of the favorite practices of those who practice external control psychology.

Think about a time when you were criticized. Remember the basic needs discussed earlier? The odds are you were not feeling a sense of belonging, at least at the moment of the criticism. What about power? It's hard to feel competent and successful when you are being criticized. Freedom? If a person in authority was criticizing you, you didn't consider just walking out because the consequences might have been particularly costly, so you were left with very little freedom. Finally, there is the need for fun. It is hard to have fun while someone berates you. When you are being criticized, then, it is virtually impossible to satisfy your basic needs.

As destructive as criticism is, strong relationships can tolerate some of it. Keep this in mind, though: criticism *never* improves the relationship. In my opinion, the relationship that most closely approximates the ideal is my relationship with my wife. In over 30 years of marriage, I have *never once been helped by my wife's criticism!* And *my criticism has never helped her!* It is true that sometimes our relationship has grown stronger after some harsh words, but the criticism itself never helped.

A strong marriage can withstand some criticism, but what about relationships at work? If criticism can destroy a marriage (as it has in many cases), imagine how easily it can destroy a relationship between you and an employee. The result is a marked decrease in morale and productivity, something no organization can afford.

Taking Time to Make Real Change

Creating healthy, productive connections with employees takes a lot of time. New managers may need to spend considerable time building strong connections with their employees. It may seem that lead management is a time-intensive process, and this is a legitimate concern for busy managers who are understandably focused on organizational success. Trust me: building and maintaining a positive work relationship with your employees is a wise investment. The time it takes will pay handsome dividends in the long run, allowing you to supervise efficiently, teach effectively, mentor more successfully, and inspire employees to do high-quality work. The result will be a more successful company.

In the beginning of a working relationship, it is necessary to spend considerable time building a positive environment. At that point, lead management appears slow and laborious. Once the environment has been firmly established, however, you will spend only a fraction of your time maintaining a strong working relationship with your employees.

If you are concerned about time, think how effective it would be if your entire management team adopted a lead management approach. When you work in a system where all supervisors practice lead management, a positive environment perpetuates itself. Your employees will work hard and do their best because of the culture and climate that you created in your workplace.

The Process

Your questions and strategies will be different depending on whether you are supervising, mentoring, or dealing with a problematic employee. I present the lead management process here in one typical sequence, but note that the order in which you cover these points is flexible. You may find it easier to follow this sequence until you become comfortable. Over time, you will develop a flexible approach that you can tailor to each situation.

It is important to acknowledge the importance of personal style. Take the following process and bring it to life by incorporating it into your style. Just as we share the same basic needs but develop a unique quality world, all of us practicing lead management use the process in ways that reflect our individuality.

Clarifying Goals

Whether you are supervising, mentoring, or managing a problem, it is essential that employees identify their goals. Employees need a clear sense of what is in their quality world. Remember that we are driven by our quality-world pictures, so we need to know exactly what we want in order to take effective action. Employees who are unclear about their goals do not engage in the decisive action needed for the high-quality performance you desire. It may difficult to believe, but many employees are unaware of what they *want* from their jobs. During the interview process they knew they wanted to be hired, but little beyond that. Their lack of clarity about professional goals limits their performance on a daily basis.

There are lots of ways to help employees clarify their professional goals. The most direct is to simply ask them, "What are your professional ambitions now that you are a part of our organization?" This is certainly a reasonable question, but don't be surprised if you encounter uncertainty and multiple or superficial answers.

Managing "I Don't Know"

Managers frequently encounter employees who say they simply don't know what they want. If this happens to you, perhaps you haven't yet established a sufficiently strong relationship for the employee to share his or her professional aspirations. Alternatively, if you are an action-oriented person who likes to get things done, perhaps you may be so focused on moving forward that you have neglected to build a strong work relationship. Many employees manifest their discomfort when asked what they want by simply saying, "I don't know." While you are looking into the future, they are still trying to determine if they can trust you.

When we reveal what we really want, we leave ourselves vulnerable. Until I know I can trust you, I will be reluctant to tell you what I want. If I tell you that I hope to move into a management role, you may see me as too aggressive or overconfident. If I tell you I'm just happy to be working here and want to do well in my current position, you may see me as too passive. My goal is for you to perceive me positively, and I'm not sure what you want to hear. The safe route is to say, "I don't know."

Only a strong, positive connection based on trust will overcome this roadblock. If I believe that you are here to help me—that you won't laugh at or criticize me, and you will help me achieve success—then I might be willing to answer the question: "What are your professional goals?"

Occasionally, there are employees who really are out of touch with what they want. This is most common with veteran employees who are underperforming. In these rare cases, it is helpful to flip the question to a negative: "If you don't know what you want, can you identify what it is that you *don't* want?" If they answer, "Well, I don't want to lose my job," ask, "Will being more productive at work help?" In this way, you move forward positively and collaboratively, creating a reasonable goal for the employee to become an asset to the organization.

When you ask employees about their professional goals, don't assume that what they tell you necessarily represents what matters most to them. It's not uncommon for people to test the waters by giving a superficial answer. Different managers have their own ways of dealing with this issue. I tend to accept "safe" goals early in a work relationship, provided that they support the mission of the organization and help the employee move forward. I suspect that the employee is consciously or nonconsciously trying to figure out whether I can help them succeed. As I help them develop competence, they gradually trust me enough to disclose what else they want to do to grow professionally and contribute to the organization.

Managing a List of Goals

Young, enthusiastic employees may provide you with an extensive list of goals. When this occurs, help them prioritize. This process helps create a need-satisfying work relationship. I would say something like this:

"It sounds like you have an idea of some of the things you'd like to achieve within the organization. You have a lot of potential and I'd like to help you, but first you have to decide where to begin. If you try to do too many things at once, you'll be spread too thin and have less success than if you focus on one area at a time.

"First, is there something that needs to be taken care of before you move to something else? It might not be the most important thing, but it's the essential first step that must be taken. If not, then where would you like to begin? What appeals most to you? All I need from you is the commitment that you'll give this your best effort."

Talking this way creates a need-satisfying environment and fosters a positive work relationship with your employees. By asking where they would like to begin, you provide freedom. By endorsing their decision of where to begin, you communicate that they are competent and know how to move forward. Finally, when you tell them you want them to achieve professional success, you address the universal need for belonging.

Exploring Goals

When employees identify professional goals, it is often useful to explore what need or needs they relate to. When they say that they want to be successful, ask them how their lives would be different if they were more competent. What would they have that they don't have now? Their answers will provide you with insight as to what they hope to satisfy through better achievement on the job. You may hear about pleasing people (connecting), proving they can do more challenging work (power), being given more latitude in job assignments (freedom), or the joy of learning something new (fun).

Another reason to have employees identify how their lives would be better if they were more professionally successful is that *talking about something we value increases our motivation.* Employees who talk about the increased freedom they will experience when their work skills improve are more likely to sustain their effort than are those who are unaware that professional success is personally satisfying.

In workshops, I often ask managers what needs are satisfied by supervising. Participants may have thought they valued their role because of the flexibility it offers (freedom), only to discover that they really value working in a group where people genuinely *care* about one another (connecting and belonging). Others discover that they are competent professionals who have positively touched the lives of many people (power).

What about you? If you were to leave your job, what would you lose in terms of needs-satisfaction? If you share your thoughts with colleagues, don't be surprised if they meet different needs through managing. Two people can successfully engage in the same activity for very different reasons. There's nothing wrong with supervisors who say that they value the freedom their roles allow, provided they help employees grow and learn.

"What Are You Doing?"

Once professional goals have been identified, determine what steps the employee has already taken. The generic lead management question is, "What are you doing to achieve your goals?" Your objective is to help employees consciously explore their behaviors. It is important that the process not become adversarial. A conversation that includes a lot of questions runs the risk of sounding like an interrogation. If that occurs, it will weaken your relationship and your effectiveness.

Turning questions into statements can help. For example, "What kind of things have you tried?" can be rephrased as, "Tell me some of the things you've tried." "What else?" can become "That's interesting; tell me more." Of course, asking questions can communicate interest and involvement, too. As you practice the process more intentionally, listen to yourself. Does your communication style strengthen or weaken the working relationship with your employees?

I often tell people that part of my job is to ask questions, identifying my role. I tell them their job is to decide which questions they will answer. This clarifies our roles, gives the other person freedom, and prepares them for the questions that follow.

Studies repeatedly show that words are less important in effective communication than tone of voice and body language. Is your tone inviting and involving, communicating that you want to help your employees be productive and satisfied at work? What about your body language? Do you appear interested, involved, caring, bored, judgmental? Think about qualities you value and add them to your repertoire to enhance your communication skills.

Self-Evaluation

One thing that distinguishes lead management from traditional approaches is the concept of self-evaluation. After identifying both the goals and implemented strategies, ask employees to evaluate their effectiveness: "Does your current approach have a reasonable chance of helping you achieve your goals responsibly, both now and in the long run?" There are three separate issues that this question addresses:

- Simple evaluation, or self-evaluation in the most general sense. This part of the question simply asks: "Is your strategy working?"

- Responsibility. An employee may identify his behavior as "successful" if he continually arrives late as long as he completes all his work. Such behavior is not responsible, however, because workers who continually arrive late negatively impact morale. Success without responsibility is not acceptable in the workplace if you want to build a quality organization.

- Long-term consequences. Self-evaluation asks employees to consider the ramifications of their choices. By exploring the future, you help your employees discover that short-term success may lead to negative consequences down the road. For example, you may supervise someone with a strong need for belonging who avoids conflict whenever possible. She continually does more than her share rather than confront her colleagues, because this solves immediate problems. Helping your employee explore the long-term consequences of avoiding conflict with coworkers will help her become more competent.

Just because you allude to potential problems in the future, don't assume that your employees will automatically change. Remember that *all* behavior is purposeful and represents our best attempt at that moment to meet our needs. Simply considering potentially negative long-term consequences will not be enough to change the behavior right away. If that were the case, managing would be much easier. Insight is not all that is needed, but it can lead to a healthy discomfort that inspires change.

Self-evaluation is the cornerstone of lead management and what makes it unique and powerful. Other management approaches move from information gathering ("What do you want and what are you doing to get it?") to analysis and prescription ("This is what you need to do.") In the course of this analysis and prescription, we evaluate for the other person: "You tell me you want to succeed in this organization, but you're not doing what you need to do. Let me tell you something, and I'm only telling you this because I care about you: If you don't change your performance, you're headed for failure."

The moment we evaluate for our employees, they lose the chance to take responsibility for their own job performance. Our evaluation is counterproductive; it often invites arguing, as employees try to justify their actions. Because all behavior is purposeful and represents your employees' best attempts at that moment, they will try to convince you that they've acted reasonably. As a lead manager, you have no interest in wasting time in lengthy dialogue about what hasn't worked. You are only interested in moving in a positive direction as quickly as possible.

When you evaluate your employees' behaviors as unsuccessful or ineffective, they feel as if they have no competence (power) in that area. This lowers self-esteem and the employees are less likely to be productive. Evaluating them also makes them externalize the decision-making process, which leads to passivity. Lead managers intentionally foster responsibility and enthusiasm.

It's tempting and easy to evaluate others. From a distance, I see things more clearly than you and can identify what you are doing wrong. I enjoy telling you how ineffective your behaviors are because I get to play the role of expert (power).

As I listen to people evaluate others, I am struck by this fact: frequently, the outside evaluators are *right*. Their prescriptions for success are often sound and sensible: "You need to do your work. And remember, it isn't just the specific tasks I've assigned. It also means *thinking* about what you are doing, and how you can do it even better. Going the extra mile is just as important." The problem is that their evaluations, advice, and prescriptions are often unheard or unheeded. People will change only when *they* make the self-evaluation that their current behavior is not taking them in the direction they want to go. Paradoxically, when you evaluate for another and prescribe a remedy, continued substandard performance is appealing because defying you satisfies the need for freedom. When your employees are more driven by freedom than competence, your suggestions will almost always be ignored.

What Motivates Change?

When we evaluate others and prescribe behaviors, we are trying to *make* them do something. While we may do it "for their own good" and for the good of the company, it still involves coercion. Why do people change their behavior? There is an identifiable process that explains why people choose to change behavior. The specifics vary from case to case, but the process remains constant.

Consider the actively drinking alcoholic. Many of us are familiar with situations where loving family members, coworkers, and a host of others try to *make* the alcoholic stop drinking. I am not saying that our efforts don't matter, but the alcoholic will not give up drinking until he makes the evaluation that alcohol is causing him so many problems that he needs to live his life another way. Our efforts are important, but we cannot *force* another to give up drinking. The process of recovery begins only when the alcoholic "hits bottom" and decides that drinking is not working. Our efforts can accelerate the process somewhat, but the alcoholic still needs to self-evaluate.

Most people accept that the alcoholic will only stop drinking when *he* makes that decision. Many would say that self-evaluation alone is not sufficient, and that support like counseling or Alcoholics Anonymous is required. But virtually everyone agrees that self-evaluation is a necessary component in the change process. The same is true when discussing change in job performance.

We accept that an alcoholic needs to self-evaluate before he will change his behavior, yet we continue to try to change our employees without giving them the opportunity to self-evaluate. We try to *make* them perform better, work harder, be responsible. We listen to endless chatter and read scores of books about how to motivate others, as if motivation comes from an outside source. As a lead manager, you don't make employees do anything or motivate them at all; rather, your responsibility is to nurture their ability to honestly self-evaluate so they can take advantage of the internal motivation driving all of us. Your objective is to unleash their innate drive to be competent, productive, and successful.

I frequently do what others want. A colleague asks me to do something for her and I comply almost automatically. Over time, I may come to believe that she *makes* me do certain things, but that's not the case. I cooperate because I instantaneously make the evaluation that doing what my coworker asks satisfies my drive to connect. Acting cooperatively with coworkers helps me enjoy my job. As habitual as it may be, my behavior is driven by my internal evaluation, not from some outside force.

The language of irresponsibility permeates our vocabularies: "I have to get up early tomorrow," "I have to go to work," "I don't want to go to this party, but I really need to." Each time we communicate in this way, we perpetuate the myth that we are externally controlled. Since *most* of us communicate this way, is it any wonder that many of our employees develop irresponsible orientations?

Consider all the "have to, need to" statements you make and check out just how true they are. Do you really *have* to get up early or go to work? Almost assuredly, you do not. That's not to say that you *shouldn't* get up early or go to work, or that there will be no consequences if you arrive late to work or take a day off. Still, such statements suggest a failure to recognize that you are making choices to live your life in a particular way. Acknowledging that you don't *have* to get up early but that you *choose* to for some very good reasons doesn't mean you will always enjoy doing it, but it will help you to realize that you constantly make choices about how to live your life.

Sometimes we choose certain behaviors so regularly that we forget they are choices. They seem to just "happen" to us and we believe they are caused by outside sources. Take the behavior of getting angry. You may have seen a manager become angry when someone's job performance was substandard. Before I learned internal control psychology, I would sometimes say, "My son makes me angry when he comes home late." Angering is not a behavior I am proud of, so I preferred to blame my son for my anger, rather than take responsibility for it myself. But you know what? My son doesn't *make* me anything. He doesn't *make* me angry. He doesn't *make* me happy. All he does, like the rest of us, is *behave a certain way.* When he chooses behavior that is different from what I want, it's easy to tell people he makes me angry; when he chooses behavior that matches what I want, it's easy to say he makes me happy. In both cases, I am wrong.

If you want to put these principles into practice and not just read about them, pay attention to your language. Do you say that you believe in freedom and responsibility but use the language of irresponsibility and imprisonment? How often do you say you "have to" when you don't? How often to you say other people "make" you happy, angry, frustrated, etc.? Do you grant power to others by saying that they "push your buttons"?

Think of a time when someone insisted that you do something and you refused. It's irrelevant what the situation was. If you can remember just one time when someone insisted that you *had* to do something and you didn't do it, you have concrete evidence that you cannot be *made* to do anything. In that situation, you decided it was more need-satisfying to behave differently from how you were told you *had* to behave. Every decision you make, large or small, follows the same process. You quickly, often nonconsciously, self-evaluate and behave in a way that is most needs-satisfying at that moment.

The Cost of Fear

If your employees are unwilling to make an honest self-evaluation (even when it's obvious to you that they are doing substandard work), it usually is a signal that your relationship with them is not strong enough. Employees honestly self-evaluate in environments they perceive as safe and conducive to success. If they believe the environment is hostile or even neutral, they will be less likely to take the risk associated with self-evaluation. From an internal control perspective, they are driven to survive (i.e. keeping their job by denying there is a problem) rather than driven to be powerful by admitting to problems and developing new competencies.

Relationship Is the Key

When I have a positive connection and communicate to employees that I care about them, they will honestly self-evaluate. Lead managers need their employees to believe them when they say: "I'm here to help you become satisfied and productive employees." If they believe you and trust you, virtually all workers will flourish.

When employees acknowledge that their current behaviors are not helping them be as successful as they would like to be, ask them a question like, "Want to try something different?" At this point, especially if you are greeted with anger, sarcasm, or frustration, remember: all people are doing the best they can. It would not be unusual for an employee to say something like, "Don't you think I'd try something else if I could? I don't know what else to do!" The unskilled manager can easily stumble here. If you're not careful, you might find yourself saying, "Look, I'm trying to help you! You're the one who has just *admitted* that you're not doing your job very well. I don't need your attitude. When you decide to treat me with the respect I deserve as your boss, I'll be ready to talk."

As the lecture continues, all hope of facilitating positive change goes out the window. I have seen this happen many times: well-intentioned but unskilled supervisors are sidetracked by the emotionalism of the employees they're trying to help. Be prepared for the emotional onslaught you will likely encounter and do not deviate from your goal of helping employees become more successful. Say something like, "I understand that you are frustrated and I'm sure you've tried everything you could think of. But my question is still the same: want to try something else? If we can figure out something together that we agree has a good chance of working, do you want to give it a shot?"

Acknowledge frustration, anger, or whatever other emotion is present. Although you shouldn't spend unnecessary time on negatives, connections are strengthened when you acknowledge them.

Building a Plan to Change Behavior

Building a successful plan to improve job performance takes effort. The best plans are:

- Short

- Simple

- Not contingent upon the behavior of others

- Measurable

- Attainable

The most important characteristic of a plan is that it is attainable. If you develop a plan that is too easy, that's a problem easily rectified. What you don't want is failure, especially with employees who are struggling. Beware of employees who have a long history of substandard performance, as they tend to develop grandiose plans. Desperate to please, they are prone to promising more than they can deliver. A good lead manager helps employees create a realistic, attainable plan, maximizing the chance of success.

Make plans that are not contingent on the behavior of others. If I say I'll do something *as long as someone else does this or that,* I have forfeited my power and autonomy. If the other person doesn't come through, I have a built-in excuse for my failure. Lead managers help employees succeed *regardless of what others do.* A plan that is contingent upon the behavior of others perpetuates the belief that success is the result of forces over which I have no control. I would rather develop a modest plan that relies on no one but the employee than a more substantive plan that is contingent on the behavior of others. Professional success requires that employees learn to act in a responsible way regardless of what others choose to do.

Who creates the plan? The lead manager gives as little help as possible and as much as necessary when creating a plan with an employee. Ideally, plans should come from the employees, but they frequently need help devising them. Help may take the form of brainstorming ideas or may be more directive, depending upon the employee's resourcefulness.

Imagine you are working with an employee and you have information that would be helpful to her as she makes plans. It would be irresponsible for you to withhold that information. Your role is to give her access to as much relevant information as possible so she can make the best possible decision.

Sometimes you will work with people who are less creative or resourceful, who can't develop a plan independently. Under those conditions, I am comfortable brainstorming, creating several possibilities from which to choose. Develop options, but encourage the employee to choose—an essential aspect of their professional responsibility. If you simply make a suggestion, the employee may experience immediate success, but will not grow professionally and develop increased responsibility.

Whenever possible, develop a contingency plan. Ask "What will you do if ..." questions to promote thinking and help employees understand that things don't always go as planned. The business world is volatile and those who are successful always have a back-up plan. Success is determined by how we handle things when they don't go the way we expect.

Once a plan is committed to, you need to check on how successful the employees have been. This enhances your connection, communicating to the employees that you care enough about them to find out whether they followed through on their plans. Follow-up discussions provide another opportunity for employees to self-evaluate and grow. It may be tempting to praise or punish, depending on how successful they have been. Try to give up the carrot and stick and encourage employees to evaluate their own performance.

Imagine someone you supervised told you he was going to complete a project by Tuesday. When you meet, he shows you the work, which is complete and well done. The traditional approach to management is to praise the employee for doing what he said he would do. Praise feels good but *it is not as valuable as self-evaluation* if you want your employees to internalize a sense of industry and responsibility.

The lead manager asks, "What do you think about your work?" This allows employees to publicly take ownership and articulate that they feel good about themselves for having performed successfully. The manager affirms what the employees have said, but always asks for a self-evaluation *before* externally evaluating.

If employees fail to do what was planned, criticizing only compromises whatever connection you have developed and minimizes the chance of future success.

Instead, calmly say something like, "When we spoke last time, your plan seemed like a good idea. Does it still seem worthwhile to you or not?" Assuming the answer is yes, say, "OK, if it's still a good idea, let's figure out something that *will* work." Then build a better plan. Berating your employees for their failures only wastes time. If the plan no longer seems appropriate, revise it.

Conclusion

Lead managers help employees identify their professional goals, examine what they've done to be successful, and evaluate their own performance. You can use this process every day, making lead management both practical and usable. Help your employees expand their horizons so they want to produce high-quality work. With an internally motivated workforce that wants to be successful, we can create the thriving, prosperous organizations we envision.

Reflection

To supervise effectively, develop a strong working relationship with your employees. Workers who believe you care about them are more likely to produce the high-quality work we want. Without a strong connection, workers will find it easier to take short cuts in every aspect of their jobs. A strong working relationship involves helping workers set goals, self-evaluate, and plan effectively.

CHAPTER 4

▼

AN INTRODUCTION TO A QUALITY COMPANY

Are employees in your company driven by fear? Do they see you as a leader or a boss? Is the emphasis on "getting the job done" or "doing the job well"? Do employees evaluate their work for quality?

Dr. W. Edwards Deming, a noted industrialist and tireless promoter of quality, is considered by many to have been the most influential individual in Japan's rise to economic power after World War II. At that time, the Japanese had a reputation for shoddy workmanship. Deming convinced them that he could teach them to create quality products that the world would buy. They listened, and soon Japanese products became models of quality. Dr. William Glasser, the creator of choice theory, studied Deming's complex system and identified the three essential elements that form the heart and soul of every quality company:

1. Eliminating coercion and driving fear out of the workplace

2. Focusing on quality

3. Instituting a system of self-evaluation

Each organization that pursues increased quality is unique. What is appropriate in one setting may be counterproductive in another. There is no recipe for quality. If there were, quality could be achieved by simply copying what works. You can learn a lot by studying successful organizations, but don't think you will replicate their achievements by simply following their blueprint. To build a quality company, you must chart your own course. If you don't, the best you can achieve is mediocrity.

Eliminating Coercion and Driving Fear Out of the Workplace

Too many companies are coercive, with employees toiling under the cloud of fear. When you coerce others, it is difficult for them to feel powerful and free. Typically, they resent you, frustrating their drive to connect. Not surprisingly, there is little fun. The coercive workplace is decidedly unsatisfying and quality work is almost never done. This all but guarantees organizational failure.

As discussed in Chapter 3, nobody *makes* us do anything. Crusaders, hunger strikers, and others who sacrifice their lives for causes to which they're committed prove this point. In ordinary circumstances, however, people do successfully *coerce* each other. You may have power over me and order me to do something. While I could defy you, it would be unwise, perhaps costing me an anticipated promotion or even my job. I do what you require, but because my needs have been frustrated, I do just enough to get you off my back. My objective is simple and specific: do enough to get you to leave me alone. At most, coercion leads to compliance. I do my best work only when I find it need-satisfying.

In Chapter 3, I highlighted the importance of developing plans that are attainable. Keep this in mind as you work to eliminate coercion in your company. A hurried attempt to get rid of all coercion immediately would be disastrous. Instead, adopt a measured approach to management reform. Create an attainable plan for yourself. Identify one or two situations where you could be just as effective without being coercive. Begin there. Don't push any further. If you commit to this course of action, you will slowly and successfully minimize coercion. Less coercion will mean less fear in the workplace, increased employee satisfaction, and increased productivity.

Remember to eliminate coercion without sacrificing your effectiveness. Coercion is purposeful. If you sacrifice effectiveness in an effort to be less coercive, you will become frustrated and go back to coercion in a hurry, probably with increased energy and anger. If you give up coercion *without* sacrificing your effectiveness, you will shed your coercion easily.

Consider the following questions:

- Do your employees fear you?

- Do you fear some of your colleagues?

- Do supervisors fear upper management?

- Does upper management fear anyone?

If you answered "yes" to any of these questions, you have a place to begin. Start building an environment where fear has been driven out. In a fear-laden system, mediocrity rules; in a system where fear has been eliminated, quality can flourish. Which environment are you creating?

Boss Management

Traditional management can be described as "boss management." Bosses are obeyed because they have power over their subordinates. They capitalize on fear and coerce workers into doing what is expected. Employees do what they are told because to do otherwise would be to invite unpleasant consequences. Fearing negative evaluations, most employees grudgingly conform, operating on a survival level much of the time. Workers driven by survival are not interested in becoming more competent and building a quality organization. They are simply "working for the weekend."

In many companies, supervisors not only boss, but are bossed from above. Upper management uses the same coercive behaviors with middle management with the same results. At most, bossing leads to compliance. If unthinking conformity is all you need to be successful, it may be appropriate. Organizations that need only compliance to prosper can use a boss-management approach. If, however, there are gradations of quality and you need the best your employees can give you in order to prosper, then the traditional boss management model is inadequate. If the goal is quality, then bossing simply doesn't work. To achieve quality, lead management must replace boss management.

Lead Management

Whereas a boss *tells you* what to do, a leader *shows you*. A boss is intent on assessing blame and controlling workers by rewarding and punishing; a leader helps each worker contribute positively so the organization thrives. Leaders make it clear that their job is to help employees do *their* jobs better, to teach them relevant skills, and to help them become more valuable to the organization.

Effective lead managers have tremendous energy and help others become more energized. They engage their employees and articulate a clear, shared vision of quality. They communicate the following messages:

- We are stronger and more successful with your input.

- Your input is valued, even though we will not always move in the direction you suggest.

- We want you to think about how to make this organization stronger.

- Your ideas will always be heard.

Less skilled lead managers are tentative and too cautious. Fearful of offending anyone, they try endlessly to build coalitions and reach compromise so that there are no hurt feelings. The result is an organization that is always treading water. The organization does not change much from year to year, but it is not a healthy conservatism driven by a desire to progress wisely; it is a spineless conservatism, fueled by indecisiveness and a lack of vision. Over time, employees in these companies lose energy and enthusiasm. The workplace becomes deadly instead of vital, evolving, and constantly improving.

Focusing on Quality

In a successful organization, the emphasis is on the quality of the work done and the quality of the interaction among employees.

Those unfamiliar with internal control psychology often wonder whether employees really want to improve the quality of their work. They are used to traditional management systems where employees produce work that is evaluated by someone else. In such settings, the evaluation process serves to identify success and failure—a time-intensive and redundant process, since employees usually know before any formal assessment if they have done quality work.

Effective lead managers inspire their employees to be successful while supporting the mission of the company. Everything we do should be consistent with that, and we should modify or abandon practices that are not.

Quality work requires the following components: a set of company standards, the best effort of employees, and an ethic of continuous improvement. Engaging in quality work feels good because we satisfy our needs, particularly for power and competence. As you reflect upon your personal and professional accomplishments, you probably feel good about yourself. You worked hard. You may have sacrificed. Perhaps you persevered even when things were difficult and it would have been easy to quit. These accomplishments feel good because they added quality to your life.

Instituting a System of Self-Evaluation

Universal self-evaluation is essential to achieve organizational excellence. In traditional, boss-managed companies, evaluation is an external, top-down affair. Most people work in companies like this. Identifying the limitation of the traditional management model is easy when looked at from an internal control psychology perspective. Traditional evaluation is external: a manager evaluates you. Because the manager has legitimate power over you (i.e. the power to give you a poor performance evaluation or fire you), you conform enough to ensure your professional survival. Over time, an interesting dynamic evolves. Compliant behavior helps employees maintain their jobs, but grudging compliance runs counter to our genetic instruction to be free. An internal system of checks and balances drives our employees to conform enough to survive while rebelling enough to maintain their autonomy. The result is that work generally gets done, but *quality* work is rare.

In extreme cases, there is not even minimal compliance. Some employees have such a strong need for freedom that they have difficulty doing what they are told to do even if it is "for their own good." Employees like this are likely to have many conflicts with their boss managers and do poorly in systems based upon external evaluation. Likewise, creativity is virtually nonexistent in boss-managed organizations, because creativity requires an environment where employees are comfortable taking risks. Since quality and creativity go hand in hand, the limitations of a boss-managed system are obvious.

You can be reasonably assured that your employees will put forth maximum effort when they determine that performing well will add quality to their lives. This is why it is imperative to incorporate self-evaluation into your work environment. To be successful over the long haul, companies must be managed in a way that supports the internal motivation of their employees.

Self-evaluation builds an internal locus of control, contributes to a sense of personal power, and promotes responsibility. A lead manager expects employees to evaluate their own efforts first, but self-evaluation alone is inadequate. It is easy to imagine the following scenario: You ask an employee to evaluate her work before you see it. The employee wants to do well. Having been given no model of quality to compare to her efforts, she is left to her own devices to figure out whether she's doing quality work. She forwards the work to you for your feedback. As her supervisor, you become frustrated that she would show you something so obviously devoid of quality.

You can circumvent this problem by discussing with employees what quality work looks like before having them self-evaluate. Develop a shared understanding of what quality will look like in each situation. Show models of quality when appropriate. Provide checklists or descriptions so that employees can engage in useful self-evaluation when they have completed a task. Self-evaluation requires skill to be done well. A good lead manager provides employees with the skills needed to engage in productive self-evaluation.

When self-evaluation incorporates models, examples, standards, and useful feedback, managers embrace it. When I discuss these issues in workshops, participants readily see that self-evaluation supports quality. Managers appreciate how this is applied in the workplace. Everything goes well until I remind them that productive self-evaluation only occurs when coercion has been virtually eliminated and fear has all but disappeared.

Imagine your supervisor announces that your performance evaluation is going to be handled differently this year. "This year I am going to leave you a blank evaluation form," she says. "I want you to complete it in the next week. We'll arrange a time to talk, compare notes, and discuss how things are going."

Assume that you trust your supervisor and believe that her goal is to help you become a more skilled and competent member of the organization. Because you perceive her as a facilitator of your professional growth and someone you do not fear, you will likely self-evaluate in a way that will help you become more competent. You are driven by your need for power and competence and self-evaluate to help you meet that need. When you meet the following week, you might say, "There are a number of things I do well. One area where I could improve involves getting back to potential clients in a timely way. I'm so focused on my initial contacts that I sometimes put off follow-ups longer than I should."

Now, change the scenario to something that may be more familiar. Imagine that you fear your supervisor. She has portrayed herself as "the boss" and made the bottom line clear on numerous occasions. You both know that you are "easily replaced." She asks you to self-evaluate as part of your performance evaluation. You realize that any admission of weakness will be used to build a case against you. The need for survival (retaining your job) trumps the need for power (increased professional competence) and you say something safe: "I've given a lot of thought to this, but haven't been able to identify any weaknesses. Like all of us, I constantly strive to improve. Of course, if there's an area you'd like me to work on, I'll be glad to do my best, as always!" The presence of fear leads you to downshift from competence to survival, and the evaluation process does nothing to help you grow professionally.

Do you want your employees driven by the need to survive or the need to be competent? The quality of your relationship with your employees and the presence or absence of fear will determine how they self-evaluate. If you have been a manager who has created an environment filled with fear, you can start using lead management now.

This isn't just a theory. This isn't idle talk. This goes to the kind of supervisor you want to be. If your workplace is characterized by fear, what can you do now to create a work environment that supports increased productivity? Do your employees see you as a coach who is there to help them become more skilled in their job? Do they see you as someone to be feared, to get past, someone irrelevant to their professional growth and development? How do you *want* them to see you? How will you create an environment where productive self-evaluation can flourish? I encourage you to give these questions serious thought.

Reflection

Employees do their best work when fear is driven out of the workplace. In a quality organization, the focus is always on doing our best work, not simply on getting the job done quickly. Setting standards and having workers evaluate their own work leads to increased quality and productivity. Implementing the practices outlined in this chapter will help you be a leader instead of just a boss. Which would you rather be?

CHAPTER 5

▼

CREATING INDIVIDUAL GOALS

Have you created a personal and professional mission statement? Can you articulate exactly what you want for yourself, personally and professionally? Would you be a more effective supervisor if you had a clear vision of what you expect from yourself as a professional?

The most important person in inspiring quality in your company is *you*. Regardless of your role in the organization, don't shift the focus onto someone else. When you do, you adopt an external orientation rather than an internal orientation, abdicating responsibility and giving away personal power. Don't be passive, waiting for others to lead. Everyone is essential to build a quality company.

I am not suggesting that you violate the chain of command or encouraging you to work at cross-purposes with other managers or those above you. I am urging you to actively inspire quality in your company in a way consistent with your role in the organization. Given the scope of your authority, do what you can to make your company more successful and inspire the employees you supervise.

You first need to develop a picture of a quality company and how you would conduct yourself in such an organization. This can be tricky. Sometimes we need a highly defined map. Other times, something less precise serves us better. At this point, you need something to point you in the right direction, but too much detail will be counterproductive. Let me explain.

If a management team wants to pursue quality but chooses to be intentionally vague about the specifics, all team members can comfortably move in the same direction. Building something together will strengthen their professional relationships, and they will develop into a cohesive, unified group. Each manager initially being less specific increases the likelihood of the full management team ultimately embracing a highly defined, specific goal. If each manager begins with a highly defined goal, each will be working in isolation and invested in a narrow vision. Isolation will not lead to quality because a quality company relies on a group collaboratively forging a shared vision.

To inspire quality in your company, look within instead of talking about the "company" like it is something disconnected from you. Decide exactly what you expect to do and to get from being a manager. We behave purposefully to satisfy our needs. How does managing help you meet yours?

Belonging or Connecting: Do you have satisfying relationships at work? Is work a place where you seek to meet your need for belonging? Successful lead managing requires you to build strong working relationships with your employees. If you aren't a "people person," it may be more difficult for you to inspire others to do quality work. This doesn't mean you can't be an outstanding manager, but it is essential that you appreciate the importance of relationships in a quality organization. Effective managers with a high need for power and a relatively low need for belonging still foster the positive professional relationships that characterize successful organizations because they understand that strong professional connections improve job performance.

Power or Competence: People work for more than money. Work helps us to meet our need for personal power and competence. Most managers have a high need for power. Do you seek to gain power over others, or to help your employees succeed and contribute to the company? Which kind of power will inspire your employees and lead to a quality organization? Do you make a meaningful contribution to the organization? Has your company been enriched by your efforts? Contributing at work gives meaning to our lives.

Freedom: By its very nature, work involves a willing sacrifice of freedom. Still, some employees feel free and others feel trapped. What is it like for you? Do you perceive work as a restrictive place, or as somewhere you can use your creativity and experience freedom? As a manager, do you intentionally foster an atmosphere where your employees enjoy some freedom while remaining productive and focused on the task at hand?

Fun: Do you enjoy yourself at work? Is there joy in what you do? Do you laugh with your colleagues? Is it bitter laughter, steeped in cynicism, anger, and sarcasm, or pure laughter, drenched in the joy of living, working, sharing, and learning together?

As you think about these questions, you will get a clear sense of what work means to you. Here's another way to ask yourself some of the same questions: If you were to lose your job tomorrow, what would you lose other than money? Your answer will help you to identify what purpose work plays in your life.

Reflect upon these questions seriously. They are not "fluff." Many people are comfortable discussing issues as long as they are able to maintain a safe, detached position. But ideas are useless unless they are applied. It is absurd to acknowledge in the abstract that human beings have universal needs while ignoring that *we ourselves* have these needs. Reflecting upon how your job adds quality to your life is more than an intellectual exercise. It may be one of the most important things you do.

When I discuss these ideas with managers, many discover that work adds quality to their lives in ways they hadn't realized. They begin with an amorphous sense that they enjoy their jobs, but are unable to say exactly why work is satisfying. By consciously reflecting upon their goals, needs, and behavioral choices, they come to appreciate exactly why their jobs are meaningful. These managers discover that their values and behaviors as supervisors are congruent. They discover that work is meaningful because they express their individuality as they fulfill their managerial responsibilities.

Total Behavior

Although it is good to be action-oriented, some people act without adequate preparation. There is a difference between taking decisive, effective action and behaving impulsively. If you tend to act "just to get things going," I encourage you to slow down. In addition to acting, behavior includes thinking, feeling, and physiology. The decisive person will make sure that there has been adequate reflection before engaging in overt action. (After all, as you *think* through an issue, you *are* doing something.) Overt actions should be congruent with your thoughts and feelings. Notice the physiological component as well: get a "gut feeling, a bodily signal that helps you determine if a potential course of action is right for you.

When you consider behavior from several perspectives, your actions will be more effective and decisive. You will have fewer instances of being pulled in different directions. When you get uncomfortable feelings, welcome them as important signals and check all components of your behavioral system before moving ahead. Your actions will then be congruent and effective.

The Value of a Mission Statement

People with a clear vision of what they want are more successful. While knowing what you want doesn't guarantee success, it certainly helps. Visualizing success in specific circumstances maximizes the chances of making it happen. Many accomplished professionals routinely use visualization to enhance their performance.

Mission statements are posted everywhere—in businesses, in hotel lobbies, in schools, and even in fast food restaurants—but very few of us develop *personal* mission statements to help us make our way in the world. We all know people whose job performance is consistent, purposeful, and not subject to momentary whims and transient feelings. We also know people whose performances are far less consistent, who are slaves to whatever immediate concerns present themselves, and lack any sense of purpose. Those in the first group have a personal mission statement: they know who they are, what they value, and what's truly important to them. Their solid sense of self fosters a healthy consistency. They may not consciously realize that they have a mission statement, but they do. People in the second group don't have one. They may be as intelligent, as committed, as "good" as their counterparts, but they are traveling without an internal compass.

What type of person would you rather be? What type of manager would you rather be? Do you have a mission statement? Not one written by your company, but one composed by you and for you, outlining your goals as a supervisor or manager? Ask yourself: In your personal life, do you act consistently? Are your actions dependent upon your mood and whatever outside factors are present at the moment? Your answers to these questions will tell you whether you have a personal mission statement that governs your behavior. Assume you have nonconsciously developed a personal mission statement: Would it be worthwhile to articulate what governs your day-to-day behavior in writing? If so, do it now.

If you discover that you don't have a personal mission statement, there is no better time than now to create one. Until you do, you will lack the strength of character to be as effective and satisfied as possible. You owe it to yourself and everyone you interact with to create a personal mission statement that defines who you are, what you value, and what you believe in.

Developing a Professional Mission Statement

Now focus on work. What is your mission as a supervisor or manager? What do you want to accomplish in your career? What contribution do you hope to make to your company or profession?

Write down your professional mission statement. The process of developing your mission statement requires you to consider exactly what you want from your job. Someone interviewed you when you applied for the job. Somebody gave you a job description outlining what others expected of you. Your professional mission statement takes things a step further: it identifies what you expect of yourself.

Do yourself a favor and develop your professional mission statement before reading the next chapter—you might discover you would be more satisfied with another job. Better to pursue what inspires you than to spend the rest of your professional life working for the weekend.

Your mission statement is subject to change. If a mission statement is analogous to a personal constitution, remember that the U.S. Constitution is interpreted differently by many, yet provides a common framework for all Americans. Don't let the fluid nature of mission statements be your excuse for not beginning your work now.

As you develop your personal and professional mission statements, here are some fundamental questions to ask yourself:

1. What values are most important to you, both personally and professionally? Do you behave in ways that reflect these values?

2. How does work contribute to your personal identity?

3. How do you want to be remembered, both personally and professionally?

4. What kind of manager do you want to be? How would you like to be described by your employees? Your colleagues? Your superiors?

5. What contribution do you hope to make to the your company? Your community?

I encourage you to write your personal and professional mission statements before you read on.

Vision of a Quality Company

With the concepts of personal responsibility and control in mind, focus on your performance in a quality company without thinking about others, regardless of how vital a role they may play in the overall functioning of the company. In Chapter 8 we will examine how to forge a collective vision. At this point the focus is on *you*. Answer the following questions:

- What would *you* do in a quality company?

- What kind of behavior would *you* never engage in?

- What would we hear you say in a quality company? To other managers? To your superiors? To those you supervise? To clients/customers?

- What would you never say in a quality company? To your employees? To other managers? To your superiors? To clients/customers? To others?

Discuss your answers with others in your company. It's not important that they be well versed in lead management; they just need to be willing to talk about how to improve the company and make it a better place to work. After these discussions, you should be able to articulate your vision of a quality company. As much as you will be tempted to talk about what the company will be like and what others in the company will be like, focus on what *you* will do and say.

Write down your personal vision of a quality company. Remember that it is always evolving. As you gain information and talk with others, your ideas will likely change. Your vision represents your notion at any given time of a quality company and your behavior within that company.

If you have done the activities suggested in this chapter, you have begun to define yourself and identify your role within a quality company by taking action based on a solid theoretical foundation.

Reflection

Creating a personal and professional mission statement is worthwhile. A well-crafted mission statement creates clarity and a sense of purpose. Remember that your mission statement must "feel right." Being clear about your mission is essential if you want to be an effective, inspiring manager.

CHAPTER 6

▼

ACTION AND EVALUATION

What is your management style? Apart from the performance evaluations you have received over the years, have you engaged in meaningful self-evaluation? Would evaluating your own performance help you become a better supervisor?

In Chapter 5, I showed you how to develop a vision of who you want to be as a manager. That vision will serve as the standard that you'll use to self-evaluate. Consider your current behavior and reflect on the following questions:

- What exactly do you do as a manager? How would you describe your role?

- How do you behave on a day-to-day basis?

- How do you behave in a crisis?

- How do you structure your department or group of employees?

- What is your management style?

- How do you assess employee performance?

- How do you manage substandard performance and unwanted behavior?

- How do you interact with your colleagues and employees?

- How do you perceive other supervisors, managers, and senior staff?

Cursory answers will not inspire quality in your company. The best approach to these questions is to examine a typical workday and determine whether your behaviors are consistent with the mission statement you developed. If they are not, be assured that you are not alone: we are imperfect beings living in an imperfect world, and the first step to minimizing your inconsistencies is awareness. By bringing your full attention to the questions in this chapter, you will discover how aligned your behavior is with your values.

Remember that we construct our own reality. Consider a hypothetical employee. He is performing poorly, but you are confident that he would do better if he just worked harder. You inform him that he risks termination if his performance doesn't improve. At this point, he literally creates his reality of the situation. The reality he chooses will impact his behavior and play a decisive role in whether he succeeds or fails. He can choose either of the following realities:

1. **The "This is just awful" reality.** This emotionally charged way of looking at the situation generally leads to panic-driven, ineffective action. Behavior driven by unchecked emotion is characterized by considerable energy but unpredictable results.

2. **The "How can I use this information?" reality.** In this reality, information is processed rationally, not emotionally. Behavior driven by *thinking* is more likely to result in effective action that creates the future we want.

If our hypothetical employee views his situation through the "This is just awful" lens, he will probably remain unsuccessful. The nature of his failure will depend upon a number of factors. He may choose to be paralyzed by the information, or he may become disruptive and negatively impact morale. Regardless, once he creates a negative reality, his actions will almost assuredly perpetuate his failure.

On the other hand, if the employee views his situation from a "How can I use this information?" perspective, he can use the information that his professional future is at risk to his advantage. He is more apt to deal effectively with the situation and figure out what he needs to do to move forward. He will make more productive decisions, because he is rationally driven and his perceptions are less distorted by emotion.

Return to the questions at the beginning of this chapter. Can you adopt the "How can I use this information?" approach? How will this perceptual orientation change things? Will your future behavior be different when you perceive things positively? Do you believe that you can decide how to perceive reality without distorting it?

You are being asked to decide whether you believe you are controlled by external events, or can determine what outside events mean and how you will act upon them. If you thought internal control psychology was just a theory, you were wrong. It's discovering who is in charge of your life.

Keeping a Log

It is hard for many of us to remember everything we actually do during the course of a day, let alone a week or a month. Start keeping a log where you write down as much as you can remember about what you routinely do in a given time period. Specifically identify what it is, when you do it, and how long you spend on it. The format you use is unimportant as long as you are acutely aware of your behavior. Sometimes, we can be so involved in what we're doing that we're oblivious to the world around us. Is it any wonder that some of your behaviors may contradict your stated values and mission? A log identifies behaviors that have become habits engaged in without conscious intent.

As you become consciously aware of what you do, compare your actions to your central values and mission. Gradually, you will become more conscious of everyday, routine behavior and develop greater mindfulness and clarity of purpose. Anything that increases intentionality furthers your growth and development and allows you to become the person you want to be, both personally and professionally.

Evaluation

To this point you have developed your goal (helped by the creation of a mission statement) and identified what you've been doing (using a log or something similar). Now it's time to determine how satisfied you are with your performance.

Self-evaluation helps us maintain those things that represent quality and to improve where we fall short. It inspires continuous improvement and growth. We take stock of where we are, affirm what we are doing well, and plan how to become more successful.

It is rare for anyone, regardless of their success and competence, to self-evaluate and not identify areas that they could improve. Competent professionals constantly seek to enhance their skills and improve what they are doing. The pursuit of excellence is necessary to remain a force in their field.

We self-evaluate whether we realize it or not, whether we want to or not. We automatically evaluate the effectiveness of our behaviors and continue or modify our performance based upon the feedback we receive from the outside world. This nonconscious self-evaluation happens regardless of whether we are familiar with internal control psychology or not. We literally cannot choose to *not* self-evaluate.

The self-evaluation I am advocating is *conscious* and *intentional*: I consciously evaluate how successful I am in a given situation by referring back to my goal and mission statement. By evaluating against the goal I have developed, I increase the chances of living a congruent life. People who live congruently align their daily behaviors with their most important personal and professional goals and values. While they sometimes face adversity, they seem less internally conflicted than their colleagues. They are often described as "centered," "solid," or "grounded." If those are words you want others to use when describing you, practice intentional self-evaluation.

Conscious, intentional self-evaluation helps you prioritize your values. It is easy to feel overwhelmed by multiple responsibilities. Self-evaluation with reference to your personal mission statement allows you to clearly see what is *really* most important. We are all familiar with stories of people who identified their priorities when faced with a tragedy. You don't need to experience disaster to develop clarity of purpose. Intentional self-evaluation provides the same clarity so you can quickly determine what *really* deserves your energy and attention.

As you log your daily activities, ask yourself: "Is my behavior consistent with my mission and my values? Will doing this help me become the manager I want to be?" The more you consciously self-evaluate with reference to your most important goals and values, the more effective you will be as a manager.

Conclusion

It may be tempting to read the questions presented in this chapter without giving them your full attention. If you want to experience increased quality, you need to spend time and energy examining your current performance and measuring it against your own standards. Self-evaluation requires effort. If you devote sufficient time and energy to it, you will become personally and professionally more successful. This process is worthwhile because it will enhance your life.

Reflection

Keeping a log represents a reliable way to get information about how things are going. Without one, it's easy to get caught up in the moment and lose sight of the more important trends that determine whether we are behaving like the managers we want to be. Have you started yours?

CHAPTER 7

▼

CREATING A PERSONAL PLAN

Have you created an action plan to be a more effective manager? Have your clarified your goals? Do you routinely evaluate your own performance?

Dr. Robert Wubbolding (1989) created a mnemonic device that you can use to self-evaluate. Remembering the call letters of the fictional radio station WDEP helps:

- W: Identify what you *Want*, the goal you have developed.

- D: Identify what you are currently *Doing* to achieve your goal.

- E: *Evaluate* your effectiveness.

- P: *Plan* to continue engaging in effective behavior and to change what is not working well.

In previous chapters, I showed you how to clarify your goals (W), identify your behaviors (D), and evaluate their effectiveness (E). Now it's time to plan what to do to become a more effective manager (P).

Maintaining Success

There are undoubtedly areas where you already manage effectively. Some people gloss over their successes and focus exclusively on improving their weaknesses, but it is essential to acknowledge your current competencies.

Your current successes are the foundation upon which you will build your future identity as an effective manger. That foundation must be maintained if it is to support you. Begin by solidifying plans to preserve the successes you already have. If you don't intentionally maintain what you do well, you will find yourself in a frustrating cycle where you achieve success after success and still feel as though you're getting nowhere. New foundations are continually built and ignored. They, too, fall into disrepair and crumble due to inadequate maintenance.

Successful people constantly evaluate, identify what works, and commit to behaviors that are effective. For example, let's say that you regularly treat your employees with dignity and respect. You may discover that you have fewer performance problems than other managers even though you supervise some employees who are potentially problematic. Over time, without a lot of conscious self-evaluation, you developed the habit of treating your employees with dignity and respect, even those with performance deficiencies. When you discover behaviors that increase productivity, commit to maintaining them.

A friend of mine who manages a successful company visited another company where he heard employees routinely saying "thank you" to one another. That simple gesture of politeness impressed him and he realized that he didn't say "thank you" often enough to his employees. He decided to start. Almost immediately, he noticed improved morale and increased productivity. That simple gesture of acknowledgement and respect paid handsome dividends.

There may be luck in developing successful behaviors. There is, however, no luck involved in intentionally deciding to maintain what works.

Involving Employees

Too many workers feel devalued, as though their opinions don't matter. Disengaged employees are working for the weekend. To inspire quality work and improve our companies, we need to regularly discuss important issues with employees. In a quality company, everyone focuses on and discusses quality. Discussions about quality need to be structured with care. You need to develop a positive relationship with your employees first, or they may suspect that you're just trying to con them into working harder. In that case, they will resist your efforts and undermine what you are trying to do. Until you establish a positive relationship with your employees, one based on trust, you will never inspire them to do the quality work necessary for your organization to succeed.

Begin a discussion about quality by saying something like this: "If this were a quality company, what would it be like? What would you see me do and hear me say? How would I behave as your supervisor? What would I hear you say and see you do? How would you perform? As we talk, let's keep our comments positive and remember our respective roles in the company." As long as you have a trusting relationship with your employees, it is appropriate to respectfully challenge their ideas.

Discussions about quality should gradually become more specific. Initially you want to develop consensus about the work environment and general job performance in a quality company. When everyone agrees on those broad parameters, then discuss specific jobs and assignments.

After awhile, it may seem that you no longer need to have discussions about quality. This is an illusion. If you stop being intentional about quality, you will regress. Before long, you and your employees will fall back into old, less effective ways. Continue to talk about quality regularly, even if the conversations are brief. When you reach this maintenance phase, continue to nourish what you have grown together.

Develop Your Action Plan

It is time to create your action plan. Like all successful plans, it should be specific, attainable, and something you can begin right away. The best plans will not be contingent upon what others do. Plan what you can do to inspire quality in your company regardless of what anyone else chooses to do.

Of course, your task will be easier if others are involved. The organization will move faster and further with more staff intentionally pursuing quality. However, as someone who practices internal control psychology, don't let your actions be determined by what others choose to do.

Clarify Your Plan

If it would be helpful to put your plan in writing, do it. It doesn't matter if you *want* to; simply decide if putting your plan on paper increases the likelihood of you becoming the manager you want to be. If writing the plan won't help, then don't waste your time. Either way, you need to clarify your plan—you need to know *what* you will do, *when* you will do it, and *how* you will evaluate your progress. Without these specifics, you will be less successful, give up more easily, and lose the opportunity to become the effective manager you want to be.

Make a Commitment

Once you've created your plan, you need to assess how committed you are to executing it. Imagine that part of your plan includes organizing a staff development workshop. Are you really going to organize the training, or are you simply going to throw the idea out as a trial balloon and see if there is interest among the employees?

Many managers develop tentative plans that lack the commitment needed to initiate meaningful change. Just as an out-of-shape person needs to commit to a program of regular and meaningful exercise and a healthy diet in order to improve health and get in shape, you need to commit to a plan that requires effort, time, and energy if you want meaningful improvement. Every supervisor wants to be effective and inspiring. The question is: "How committed are you to becoming the supervisor you want to be?"

Reflection

Without a clearly defined action plan, it's easy to spin in cycles endlessly, working hard and getting nowhere. Those who get ahead are those who have determined exactly what they want and how to get it. Having a goal is not enough; to succeed, you need to be committed and to persevere when things get tough. Are you adequately committed to being a success?

CHAPTER 8

▼

CREATING A COLLECTIVE VISION

Do you believe it's important to get virtually everyone in you organization to "buy in" to your plan? Do you avoid conflict, or do you relish a spirited exchange of ideas? Are you skilled at helping people work toward a common goal? Is that something an effective supervisor does?

In Chapter 5, I encouraged you to create your personal vision of a quality company. I suggested that you focus on your role and keep your vision for the entire company somewhat flexible. It is now time to create a *shared* vision of a quality company. Working collaboratively requires skills that many managers have never used before. Your task is to develop a fully articulated vision of a quality company that every employee will embrace. It is not enough that everyone can live with the vision. To inspire the staff, all employees must own it. Ideally, everyone will feel that their ideas have been incorporated into the companywide vision statement. Rather than being a watered-down vision eroded by compromise and concession, the ideal shared vision encompasses and transcends each individual contribution.

Managing Disagreements

Don't be alarmed when you encounter conflict as you create a collective vision. Friction is inevitable; what matters is how you deal with it. Now more than ever, you will find that practicing lead management will help you succeed.

Pay attention to how your group functions. Is there a core group of employees that dominates everything? Without quick and decisive action, the process will stall before you know it. Some employees may feel left out and disenfranchised. Those who dominate may be unaware of their effect on their coworkers. Often they are committed, energetic employees with strong opinions who get so caught up in creating the vision that they are oblivious to group dynamics. They are focused on the product, not the process. To inspire quality in your company, employees must trust the process utilized to achieve their goals. If the process is exclusionary or divisive, even unintentionally, success is unlikely. You are not moving toward quality if your vision reflects only the beliefs of a few vocal employees. You may have a wonderfully written vision, but you will lack your most important resources: the vitality, energy, and commitment of everyone in the organization.

There is usually at least one employee in a group who is especially sensitive to interpersonal dynamics, who hears the deafening silence of the disconnected. The silence informs this employee that the group is not moving as cohesively as some believe. Using lead management, this employee can get the group back together before things unravel. Suppose this employee is you, but you tend to avoid conflict and confrontation. This is your chance to grow, both personally and professionally. This is your time to act in a new, creative, and effective way. Seeing this as an opportunity to grow instead of an uncomfortable moment is choosing to perceive reality in a way that leads to new, effective behaviors. The choice is yours—literally.

As you create your collective vision, all employees, including managers, will make mistakes and act in less than ideal ways. Both managers and employees will occasionally lose their temper, but regrettable incidents will be rare and recovery will be swift if group members trust one another. Most importantly, all employees will feel free to express themselves honestly without fear of being hurt. When employees feel as if they have something to say but are afraid they may be punished if they speak honestly, the system is toxic. As a manager, it is your job to make certain that is not the case.

In almost every organization there are employees with strong opinions. These people frequently move into leadership positions. Many of them have not learned about lead management. The power of their position and of their convictions has helped them get what they want. Many have charming personalities and can articulate their ideas clearly and persuasively. While these skills are valuable, they are not sufficient for those who wish to bring out the best in those they manage.

Lead managers accept the responsibility that comes with being in charge. Because they understand that fear undermines quality work, they do everything possible to drive fear out of the workplace. They also realize that no one person is as smart as the group. With this orientation in place, lead managers creating a collective vision seek input from their employees, who in turn find that their need for power is well satisfied. This leads to increased self-esteem and fuels increased productivity.

Some years ago, my older daughter told me how good it felt to work for a supervisor who "listened." Because she knew that her ideas would be seriously considered, she was more engaged than she would have been if she were simply told what to do. Her increased productivity led to her being promoted to a management position within the company. Employees who feel valued are more productive and help the organization move toward quality.

Skilled lead managers help safeguard and appreciate our diversity while helping us forge a common vision so we move forward together without compromising our individuality and creativity. People with these leadership skills are rare, and companies with such leaders are fortunate.

Who Creates the Vision?

Who creates the vision statement of the company? Is it the sole responsibility of the CEO? Is it the responsibility of upper management? Do you involve your entire management team? Are non-management employees part of the process? While there is no one right answer to these questions, whoever is involved in creating the vision will be more invested and probably more productive. I would involve as many employees as fully as possible in the process. The more people you involve, the more time-consuming the work, but the results are worth it.

All members of an organization should be encouraged (but not required) to submit a vision statement in writing. If the number of employees is small enough, everyone can collaboratively draft the companywide vision. If numbers would make everyone's direct involvement too unwieldy, then a representative group should be convened to draft the vision statement. Putting together a representative group is a delicate issue, and if it is not handled well your effort will be wasted. I have heard about companies where senior staff members don't want to "burden" the employees with the "tedious" job of drafting a vision, so they do the work themselves. Because workers have no voice in who will represent them, they feel alienated and disconnected from one of the most important things the company will ever do.

If a company is large enough to require a representative group to put together a draft, it is essential that the employees select their representatives directly and that they trust them completely. Without that trust, the process will break down. They need to believe that whatever information they give their representatives is listened to and valued. They need to know that their individual visions of a quality company are embodied in the whole. If they trust their representatives and they believe that they have been part of creating a vision statement, even indirectly, they will enthusiastically support what is developed. Without that trust and the belief that their contribution makes a difference, they may withdraw and be less invested, and their work may be indifferent and substandard. When employees believe that their input doesn't matter, they start working for the weekend.

Gathering Feedback

Once a representative group has drafted a collective vision, present it to the entire staff as just that—a draft for them to review and evaluate. Prepare copies of the draft for each employee with a memo that says something like this:

"The task of our group has been to draft a vision that incorporates the thoughts of every employee. Our effort is ready for your review. As you look at the draft we have developed, determine if your ideas are captured in this collective vision. This draft represents our best effort, but it can be changed. If you have any suggestions to strengthen our statement, we will consider your ideas.

"Thanks for giving this draft your thought and attention. We appreciate your feedback."

Revision and Adoption

After receiving feedback, the representative group revises the draft as necessary. If significant changes have been made, the group should solicit additional feedback. If the changes are minor, it is time to ask the staff as a whole to adopt the vision statement. When you ask them to do so, say something like this:

"Will you support the following vision statement and behave in ways consistent with it? We have done our best to create a vision that honors our individuality, yet identifies common principles in which we believe. We believe our company will be stronger if each of us commits to supporting this vision statement."

Creating a companywide vision of a quality organization is not a trivial endeavor. In doing this work, you are creating your collective professional identity. Rather than reading about what you should do in a book, you are engaging in the arduous but satisfying process of reflection and self-evaluation. What you develop will be the reference point upon which future organizational decisions are made. Rather than being lost at sea and rudderless, you will make decisions by evaluating whether your actions are consistent with your collective vision of a quality company.

Creating a companywide vision of a quality company is more than just hard work—it is a creative act of responsibility. It actively engages each employee. Done well, it can energize and transform a company.

Integrating New Employees

Once a companywide vision has been adopted, it serves as the organization's constitution. Of course, over time the company will hire new employees as people retire, take new jobs, and the company grows. During the application and interview process, it is critical to share the company vision with prospective hires. Let them know this is what you stand for, what you believe in, and the reference point against which you measure your professional decisions. Before being hired, prospective employees should review your vision and affirm that they, too, will support the vision and conduct themselves in accordance with the principles that the organization most values.

Reflection

It is essential that all employees feel involved when you create a collective vision. If they believe they are only involved to "rubber stamp" what management wants, the process will fail and productivity will decline. When you involve everyone in the decision-making process, employees feel connected and important, and want to help the company to be successful.

CHAPTER 9

▼

CREATING A COLLECTIVE PLAN

Are you prepared to move toward increased quality? Will you involve your employees and show that you are a different kind of supervisor in a different kind of company?

Once the staff adopts a vision statement embodying the varied contributions of all employees, it's time to develop your collective plan of action. If you have reached this point without employees opting out, then you will be energized by your shared vision of a quality workplace.

There is tremendous power unleashed when a group has forged a vision that all employees support with enthusiasm. Developing a collective plan means everyone has a clear definition and description of their role; everybody knows exactly who does what. Carefully delineating the specifics ensures that roles and behaviors are congruent. In any large company, it is easy to develop roles that will put employees at cross-purposes. Internal consistency and constancy of purpose must be preserved, because any internal inconsistency compromises your success.

Your goal is to ensure that all roles and behaviors are complementary. Many organizations use the metaphor of an orchestra, in which each member contributes to a whole that is greater than the sum of its parts. In order to produce beautiful music, all musicians must play their part exactly as it is written. No one tries to upstage anyone else. No one steals the spotlight or seeks individual glory. Egos are held in check because there is an understanding that the desired effect—beautiful music—is only achieved when everyone works collaboratively according to their roles.

Examine all the day-to-day, routine behaviors and events that make up the workday. As you develop your collective plan, be sure that it is success-oriented. In addition to long-term goals, set attainable short-term goals, as achieving and acknowledging your short-term accomplishments fuels enthusiasm about your organization's success.

Your plan must be measurable. How will you know if your company is better in six months? Two years? Five years? Ten years? How will you evaluate your efforts? Successful companies are results-driven. Be sure that you can measure and demonstrate your success to yourself and others, including existing and potential clients and stockholders.

Reflection

The energy is palpable once employees feel involved and respected. When employees know that their voices are heard and their contributions are valued, they are capable of great things. Be certain to define roles and responsibilities to be complementary so that everyone in the organization is working toward a common goal. Moving forward collaboratively and effectively represents the fruit of your labor.

CHAPTER 10

▼

MANAGING PROBLEMATIC EMPLOYEES

Do you have some employees who are performing poorly? Would it be helpful to determine why an employee is struggling? Is it more cost-effective to help a struggling employee succeed or to hire someone new? Can you tolerate a few underperforming employees, or do you want all employees to be productive and contribute to the success of the organization?

Most supervisors are competent, motivated workers who rose through the ranks. Underperforming employees often confound them, because the very idea of not performing to capacity is completely alien. They almost always use a coercive approach with these employees, naively believing that the threat of unpleasant consequences will motivate them to behave better.

In an ideal setting, supervisors function as teachers, providing skills to workers so the company achieves its goals. The single biggest problem we face in management is that too many employees do not adequately value what we are trying to do. While we are working to make the company a success, they are simply working for the weekend.

Employees who want to be productive are a joy to supervise. Because you want the same thing, you have a partnership that makes work a satisfying experience for both of you. Some employees assimilate information and master skills quickly, while others struggle with every new task, but nearly all of them are successful when they want to be productive and learn from you. At the same time, you satisfy your own need for competence when you help eager employees develop their skills and contribute to the organization in positive ways.

Employees overcome their weaknesses with relative ease when they really want to learn how. Of course, every now and then a new employee turns up who is not especially eager to master what is required by the job. In addition to being taught how to do the job, these employees need to be managed effectively.

One important component of management involves communicating to your employees that you care passionately about your work. Unenthused supervisors cannot inspire their workers, making it impossible to achieve high quality. When we display enthusiasm for our jobs, employees sense that it is worthwhile to be as productive as possible. They begin to see work as inherently valuable rather than just something that gets us to the next weekend.

Employees are likely to be more productive when they see their contribution as relevant and important to the success of the organization. In his book *My Gift in Return* (2003), Barnes Boffey writes eloquently about the connection between relevance and high quality:

"During the Apollo space program at NASA in the Sixties, a process was designed to clarify job descriptions and responsibilities. A custodian was asked, 'What does your job here entail?' He replied, 'I am helping to put a man on the moon.' He saw the connection between his efforts and the greater good for himself and humankind; he understood his role as well as his job. He cleaned and swept and polished with an awareness that others could do their jobs better if he did his well. I would like to have worked with that man" (p. 268).

A skilled lead manager helps all workers see that their contribution matters. Help your employees transcend themselves by understanding how their work contributes to something larger. It will inspire better work.

Prevention

An effective lead manager designs need-satisfying work. Consider what you ask your employees to do. Disruptive employees are not satisfying their basic needs at work. Successful lead managers do not waste time bemoaning the fact that some employees are "high maintenance;" instead, they try to create an environment that is need-satisfying for all employees. In such an environment, disruption is rare and quality work is possible.

Ask yourself the following questions:

- If employees do what I ask, can they meet their needs responsibly?

- Is it easy for employees to satisfy the need to connect while doing what I ask?

- Do I provide them with tasks that help them increase their competence?

- Are tasks organized in a way that allows for freedom and autonomy?

- Is laughter and playfulness valued in our company? Do my employees enjoy their jobs?

If you answer all of these questions affirmatively, you will have focused and productive employees, and any problems that arise will be handled quickly and easily. By giving your employees a work environment where they can meet their needs, there is no reason for them to fail. You have created the conditions that foster productivity.

When employees cannot satisfy their needs by doing what the supervisor wants, they frequently do something else. What they do represents their attempt to satisfy an unmet basic need, but it can be disruptive and discrepant with the mission of the organization. Since dealing with problems is time-consuming and costly, it is better to intentionally structure the environment so that employees are satisfied by doing what needs to be done. That's the lead management prevention model, based on internal control psychology.

I will offer some thoughts about intervention, but prevention is always more effective. Intervention implies a preexisting problem, whereas prevention implies effective action to avoid problems. Even the best intervention pales in comparison to successful prevention.

Intervention

When employees cause problems, your objective is simple: to end the problems and have the employees resume productive work as quickly as possible. If employees cannot meet their needs at work by doing their jobs well, it will be difficult to eliminate problems and inspire your workforce to be highly productive and successful.

Think about someone you supervise who performs poorly or disrupts the workplace. Choose someone you believe has the potential to be successful. Identify exactly what you do when this employee causes a problem. Do you ignore the situation? Verbally reprimand the employee? Issue a written warning? Engage the employee in pleasant conversation, hoping it will help him or her "get down to business"? Anything else? Make a list of what you have tried, then ask yourself how well your strategies are working with this employee. Clearly your behaviors have not been successful, or you wouldn't be frustrated, so it is your job to do something different with this employee. (I am not suggesting that the strategies you've used can't be effective in other situations; we are considering your supervisory effectiveness with this one employee.) Successful managers need multiple tools in their tool box.

Before doing anything else, remember the importance of relationships. More than anything, you must either maintain the strong connection you already have with this employee or work to strengthen the connection. Without a reasonably strong work relationship, you have almost no chance of improving the situation. In the absence of a positive relationship, the most you can hope for is the minimal compliance you may get by using coercion.

When I conduct workshops, supervisors frequently tell me that they like the ideas of internal control psychology because they are "just common sense." But common sense suggests that you *avoid* problematic employees, whereas effective lead management asks that we build and maintain a strong work relationship with them. If you adhere to a "common sense" orientation, you will remain stuck in a "me-versus-them" position and somebody will have to lose. Even if you win every time, the cost will be significant. By abandoning your common sense and working on building a better working relationship with your employees, you are moving toward a "we" position where everybody gets what they need and the organization thrives.

It is often more challenging to build relationships with veteran employees than it is with new ones. Supervisors typically mentor new hires, which often leads to a strong, positive connection because both parties meet their need for power and competence. Veteran employees are typically less amenable to change. Many are wary of supervisors, having been coerced and threatened repeatedly over the years. Nevertheless, the *only* route to success is building a stronger, better relationship, as difficult and time-consuming as that may be.

If we hope to inspire quality in our companies, we must be proactive in dealing with problematic employees. What alternatives do we have? We can coerce, threaten, and punish, thus guaranteeing that our employees will never do quality work. We can fire them, but the cost of hiring and training new employees is considerable. A successful company does not spend money only to repeat a cycle of failure. Building positive work relationships is cost-effective.

Even managers who build positive connections with their employees have challenges. The next time an employee begins to cause a problem, immediately ask, "What are you doing?" using those exact words. Don't ask why the employee is being disruptive, as it will get you nowhere in this situation. Your goal is to put an end to the problem. If the employee gets back on task, the problem has been solved even if she never answers your question.

Unfortunately, I have often seen supervisors pursue the issue rather than let it go when the employee gets back to work. It sounded something like this: "Lori, I didn't ask you to get back to work. Maybe you didn't hear me. I asked you what you were doing." Keep your objective in mind: getting workers to be productive. Does it help to make more of the situation than you need to? Any action beyond what is necessary to achieve your objective is wasting valuable time. Effective lead managers don't squander time and money.

Tone of voice and body language are even more important than your words. Sarcasm is counterproductive. When you mock your employees, they feel a loss of power and freedom. One way for them to regain control, at least momentarily, is to undermine your legitimate authority by continuing to be problematic. Ask "What are you doing?" with a sense of bewilderment, as though problems are so rare that you're not exactly sure what to make of the situation.

If the problem continues, simply ask, "Is this consistent with our company policy?" In a quality company, employees have a say in performance goals and policies. Supervisors help employees see their value. Rather than having employees perceive goals and policies as annoyances, help them appreciate that expectations help us be successful and enjoy our jobs.

When employees value the goals and policies of the organization, they are less likely to cause a problem and more likely to accept redirection. Have as few policies as possible and state them clearly and positively. "In our organization, we are courteous and productive" is one that I especially like: it's brief, has both a social and a work-related component, and is stated in the positive. Virtually every problematic behavior is covered by this single, simple policy.

Your employees will likely resume productive work once you refer to the company goals and policies, especially if they were developed with their input. Problems are generally fueled by emotion; when you focus on the company policies, you are engaging the *thinking* component instead. As employees move from a feeling-dominant orientation to a thinking-dominant orientation, their behavior will most likely change for the better.

If the problem persists, there will be a temptation to resort to coercive boss management. If employees refuse to cooperate, it will require restraint not to stoop to the typical threats. The longer you resist, however, the more your employees will realize that you simply expect them to be productive and that you have no interest in berating or belittling anyone. Your graceful management of a problem will inspire greater productivity and loyalty from most of your employees.

If all else fails, it may be necessary to conduct a disciplinary conference with the employee. While you have no interest in being coercive, it is imperative that employees perform productively and responsibly. Before conferencing, however, offer the employee a short break to see if he or she can calm down and return to productive work. An immediate conference is not advisable. We are better able to resolve problems after we've had time to clear our heads. When we are upset, we are likely to choose emotionally charged behaviors. When we cool down, we are more likely to choose behaviors that are reasonable, responsible, and productive.

The conference should be brief and to the point. You want the employee to be happy and successful. You are willing to assist in any reasonable way, but you will not sanction behavior that wastes time, diminishes productivity, and interferes with the goals of the organization. You understand that anyone can have a bad day and that even our best employees can "lose it" now and then. At the same time, a chronic failure to resume productive work will result in a written reprimand, loss of pay, suspension from work, or dismissal.

Conclusion

Each company striving to inspire increased quality will face its unique challenges. No matter what they are, however, the process remains constant: everything is referred back to your mission statement. Using lead management, define an appropriate course of action, knowing that you will make changes if they will lead to higher quality. When problems arise, remember your goal is to help employees engage in productive work that helps the company achieve its goals. You have no interest in coercing or punishing your employees, but you will insist on optimal performance.

Reflection

When you are committed to lead management, you do everything possible to help employees be successful and productive. While you will not tolerate poor performance, you know it is good business to retain employees and help them succeed instead of continually hiring, firing, and retraining them. Supervisors who help struggling employees succeed serve the organization well. Would you like to be one of those supervisors?

Afterword

Since quality is an ongoing process, I have intentionally not included a typical conclusion to this book. Instead, let me offer a few thoughts in closing:

- People are internally motivated, not controlled by outside events and forces.

- Knowledge of a theory is essential, but takes us only so far.

- Practice that is built upon a valid theory results in higher quality performance.

- When employees are satisfied and immersed in high-quality work, your organization will flourish.

- To create the successful companies, we must *manage to inspire*.

Designing organizational practices based on a valid, comprehensive theory of human behavior allows us to inspire the quality we desire. Managers, supervisors, and all other employees deserve the opportunity to create a work environment that is enriching, satisfying, and highly productive. I wish you success as you continue to build an even better company.

Bibliography

Boffey, B. (2003). *My gift in return.* Chapel Hill, NC: New View Publications.

Collins, J. (2001). *Good to great: Why some companies make the leap and others don't.* New York: Harper Collins.

Connolly, M., & Rianoshek, R. (2002). *Communication catalyst.* Chicago: Dearborn Trade Publishing.

Covey, S. (1989). *The 7 habits of highly effective people.* New York: Simon & Schuster.

Crawford, D., Bodine, R., & Hoglund, R. (1993). *The school for quality learning: Managing the school and classroom the Deming way.* Champaign, IL: Research Press.

Freiberg. K., & Frieberg, J. (1996). *Nuts!: Southwest Airlines' crazy recipe for business and personal success.* New York: Broadway Books.

Glasser, W. (1998). *Choice theory.* New York: Harper Collins.

Glasser, W. (1994). *The control theory manager.* New York: Harper Collins.

Kohn, A. (1993). *Punished by rewards: The trouble with gold stars, incentive plans, A's, praise, and other bribes.* Boston: Houghton-Mifflin Company.

Sullo, R. (1999). *The Inspiring teacher: New beginnings for the 21ˢᵗ century.* Annapolis, MD: NEA Professional Library.

Sullo, R. (2007). *Activating the desire to learn.* Alexandria, VA: Association for Supervision and Curriculum Development.

Watson, J. B. (1930). *Behaviorism* (rev. ed.). Chicago: University of Chicago Press.

Wubbolding, R. (1989, spring). "Radio station WDEP and other metaphors used in teaching reality therapy." *Journal of Reality Therapy, 8*(2), 74–79.

978-0-595-43171-7
0-595-43171-2

Printed in the United States
73735LV00003B/346-384

9 780595 431717